Evaluation of Small Business Support in Post-Apartheid South Africa

Timothy Olaniyi Aluko

Evaluation of Small Business Support in Post-Apartheid South Africa

palgrave
macmillan

Timothy Olaniyi Aluko
University of South Africa
Pretoria, South Africa

ISBN 978-981-95-2863-9 ISBN 978-981-95-2864-6 (eBook)
https://doi.org/10.1007/978-981-95-2864-6

Cover credit: Maram_shutterstock

This Palgrave Macmillan imprint is published by the registered company Springer Nature Singapore Pte Ltd.
The registered company address is: 152 Beach Road, #21-01/04 Gateway East, Singapore 189721, Singapore

If disposing of this product, please recycle the paper.

Foreword

The usual approach to researching government funding for small businesses and programme evaluation often lacks strong methodological and conceptual framing. Many of the publications in this field have argued for a lack of funding, access to loans, and consequently believe that these factors impact the growth and development of small businesses in developing countries. In multicultural societies such as South Africa, after more than 30 years of democracy, the narrative of the transformation agenda, solely based on redressing past inequality, is changing towards accountability and merit-based policy in funding small businesses. This focus requires a critical analysis of data and post-1994 literature on the topic to determine patterns and understand the usage of funds. Very few studies have approached these issues in this manner, yet government and policymakers require evidence-based decision to improve grant allocation processes.

This book provides a new perspective on understanding government programmes, grant allocation and usage, and the evaluation of funding since 1994. The author argued for a new approach that considers entrepreneurial capability, previous training or experience, and evidence of accountability as part of the policy that allocates grants to small business owners in South Africa. The book highlights corruption and misuse of government support as policy problems. Likewise, the author argues that many of the beneficiaries of government funding may not have had any intention to use the funds for the objectives of the programme. Similarly, the existing policy or transformation agenda for business development in South Africa often lacks proper accountability, and in some cases, there is no straightforward feedback process on the use of financial support. In the book, the author locates the idea of accountability through the lens of culture and history. The author argued that the transformation agenda needs to shift to funding essential sectors such as agriculture and information technology that have received little attention. The book recommends that real transformation is in policy that is intentional about factors of change in the society of South Africa, which includes funding objectives that place strong emphasis on a merit-based model where only business owners who show objective evidence of reducing poverty, crime, and unemployment are funded.

This book is unique in its depth of thinking, framing, and methodological contributions, as it analysed a historical records of funding patterns for business in post-apartheid South Africa. The clarity of writing makes the book easy to read, and the author demonstrated good scholarship through this research. Therefore, this work will be helpful as a reference book for policymakers and postgraduate students who require new ideas on small business, government grants, and the evaluation of government programmes in the post-colonial era.

I appreciate the author's boldness and careful analysis of complicated issues and topics around the transformation and business development policy in South Africa.

Prof Meshach Aziakpono
Department of Economics
Rhodes University
Grahamstown, South Africa

Acknowledgements

This book project would not have been successful without the physical, moral, and intellectual support of many individuals to whom I am sincerely grateful.

I would like to express my deepest appreciation to the University of South Africa (Unisa) for providing the academic environment that enabled the successful completion of this book.

My sincere thanks go to Prof Samuel Adeyemo of the University of Pretoria, South Africa, whose scholarly guidance, critical feedback, and encouragement were instrumental throughout the research and writing process. Also, I would like to thank Prof. Meshach Aziakpono of Rhodes University, South Africa, for writing the foreword for the book.

Likewise, I want to acknowledge the opportunity to use the datasets on the https://www.gemconsortium.com website that provide great analysis for some of the issues raised in the book.

I would like to thank the language editor, Dr. Ophelie Dangbegnon, and the publishing team at Palgrave Macmillan for their professionalism and dedication to academic excellence. Your support brought clarity, precision, and polish to this publication.

Finally, I am profoundly grateful to my family, close friends, and colleagues for their unwavering support, patience, and understanding throughout this journey. Their encouragement made it possible to pursue this scholarly endeavour with both focus and resilience.

To all who contributed in visible and unseen ways—thank you.

Contents

List of Figures

Chapter 1

Chapter 4

List of Tables

Chapter 2

CHAPTER 1

The Post-Apartheid Economic Transformation in Small Business Financing

1 Introduction

The global entrepreneurial finance landscape is continually evolving, characterised by regular governmental initiatives to implement supportive interventions and programmes. Translating these well-intentioned policies into tangible benefits for business owners remains a significant challenge, especially in developing economies. The European Commission's 2014 study of the Small Business Act provides important insights into creating a supportive environment for small and medium-sized enterprises (SMEs) in Europe. This study identifies the factors that facilitate business growth in developed countries, highlighting a systematic approach to overcoming structural challenges through detailed analysis. Although various economic and political contexts influence the systemic challenges encountered throughout Europe, there is a prevailing trend to improve support mechanisms for small enterprises.

Developing nations, such as Nigeria, encounter significant implementation gaps in policies designed to support SMEs, as highlighted by Joseph et al. (2021). The implementation deficit represents a significant global challenge, especially in Africa. Research by Fielden et al. (2000) on North-West England demonstrates strategies for overcoming implementation challenges. Njue (2021) demonstrates that the Jua-kali empowerment programme in Kenya has notably facilitated SME growth, offering a counterpoint and indicating that effective implementation

T. O. Aluko, *Evaluation of Small Business Support in Post-Apartheid South Africa*, https://doi.org/10.1007/978-981-95-2864-6_1

is achievable in particular developing contexts. This study argues that human factors are critical for the effective execution of government initiatives aimed at fostering entrepreneurial development. The emphasis encompasses the policies themselves and the individuals involved in their formulation, implementation, and impact.

The analysis of the experiences of German, British, and Irish enterprises provides significant insights into the effective implementation of interventions aimed at fostering SME growth and overall economic development, as noted by Roper (1997). Charalambous et al. (2015) emphasise the essential function of state support in maintaining the sustainability of small food enterprises in Cyprus. However, despite the Philippine government's support for Southeast Asian SMEs, Filipino entrepreneurs need to increase their engagement with micro-business enterprise programmes (Abaquita et al., 2024). Globally, the governmental SMEs' terrain is defined by various strategies that provide a similarly different range of results. Countries with favourable outcomes often include well-defined implementation strategies in their fundamental policy frameworks. Moreover, prosperous countries incorporate implementation strategies into their plans to ensure positive outcomes. It has been noted that developed countries that have achieved economic transformation through small business programmes and support have adopted strategies that work. For instance, South Korea ensures that its strategies for 5-year economic development plans include helping small businesses to succeed. South Korea has used the technology transfer method and made sure that this sector is adequately funded. What is important in this plan is the accountability process. The implementation process for the plan and performance is monitored to ensure compliance with the policy (Lee, 2014). Likewise, Germany focused its policy on SMEs to drive and support innovative businesses, which means businesses that can help the country's digitalisation and internationalisation agenda are prioritised (OECD, 2019). Similarly, Singapore Industry Transformation Programme prioritised capacity development solutions for businesses that make use of digital technology (Enterprise Singapore, 2020). These examples of developed countries ensured policies support innovative solutions and businesses that can make them globally competitive. This type of strategy is important for real development yet lacking in the South African transformation agenda of 1996. It should be noted that in Africa, and particularly in South Africa, implementation problems often stem from political, historical, and cultural factors.

Attempting to provide SMEs with the required support in post-apartheid South Africa is fundamentally problematic and deeply political. The economic transformation agenda in the newly democratic South Africa, aimed at improving access for Black-owned businesses through government interventions, has not sufficiently benefited small businesses in low-GDP growth areas, mainly due to a lack of access to credit (Baloyi & Khanyile, 2022).

As such, entrepreneurship development initiatives sought to redress past inequalities. The policy objective was to use the Broad-Based Black Economic Empowerment (BBBEE) programme to improve the South African economy (Irene, 2017). The distribution of financial resources for small enterprises defines South Africa's history to some extent and is marked by the necessity of macroeconomic development following 1994. Before 1994, White minorities held great economic power, while many Black Africans were limited to working on farms owned by the Afrikaners or living in rural communities controlled by chiefs (Thaba-Nkadimene et al., 2019), where poverty and crime hampered personal development, especially for young people and women.

The apartheid government deliberately employed tactics meant to foster a sense of intellectual inadequacy within Black communities in terms of pursuing complex academic programmes, such as engineering, medicine, and other sciences. This deliberate manipulation sought to create reliance on government directives. Under such conditions, the need for simple survival—centred on obtaining basic food—shadows any dreams for entrepreneurial activities or employment creation in these areas. The noted shortfall in business establishment was not the result of only limited resources. Instead, it came from a limited knowledge base and a complicated interaction of dread around decision-making, strongly linked and mutually reinforcing elements. As Ladzani (2010) notes, historically, the terrain of small company development in South Africa was marked by the systematic exclusion of Black, Indian, and Coloured individuals from meaningful economic involvement and benefit. The turn to the post-1994 era marked the beginning of what political scholars have described as a moment of constitutional and human rights emancipation. This era granted all South African citizens, regardless of racial or gender identity, the fundamental right to participate in the democratic process and engage in economic activities, including business prospects previously denied due to limited access to essential resources or restrictive policies. This transition marked the redefining of the social and economic possibilities open to hitherto underprivileged people and a change in legal structures.

While economic inclusion through business funding is a developmental approach, the microeconomic impacts of funding are often overlooked. However, they are crucial in understanding the influence of systemic issues on the status of business enterprises in South Africa.

In the context of this book, a conceptual understanding guides thinking and argumentation that runs through the chapters. For instance, small and medium enterprises (SMEs) are examined from both historical and economic perspectives. The argument considers the history of South Africa and what SMEs mean for economic development and transformation. This reflects in the transformation policy and how the government supports business owners is structured. In South Africa, SMEs are categorised in terms of revenue and the number of employees. This determines the size of the business to determine whether it qualifies for support as defined by the policy. Small businesses usually have between 11 and 50 employees, and medium-sized companies normally have up to 200 employees. SMEs in post-apartheid South Africa mean tools of economic transformation and justice because the policy believes Black-owned business needs empowerment for inclusivity purposes. This framework guides ideas of SMEs and funding in South Africa.

However, the concept of economic transformation in South Africa is based on the idea that poverty can be reduced or eradicated if policy can focus more on local businesses and the redistribution of wealth to Black people who have been deprived of this privilege in the past. So, post-apartheid is a deliberate term to signify and point to policy direction. It means attempting to use SMEs and funding Black-owned businesses to redress the inequality of the past. As a result, financing small business ideology is a deliberate effort to use grants and, in some cases, loans to ensure that South Africans, particularly disadvantaged groups, have access to funds to open and operate businesses of their choice. What is not clear is the accountability aspect of financing and using funds given to small business owners since 1994. Accountability in the context of this book means a process that should have been established in the policy to ensure that beneficiaries can justify the use of the funds in a transparent manner. This includes the use of money to help the government reduce poverty, unemployment, and crime. Therefore, a grant is not a giveaway, nor is it supposed to be. Thus, social justice is expected through support for SMEs. This book argued that social justice cannot be narrowly defined but should embrace the principle in distributing grants in today's South Africa. As a result, the idea of a grant is conceptualised and framed differently in this book. The BBEE Act ensures that 51% ownership of businesses must be controlled by Black businesses, which is a transformation policy. However, this book reflects on merit-based grant policies and defines them as the government ensuring that it uses fair criteria in distributing social benefits to citizens.

2 Status of Business Development in South Africa

Small and medium enterprises (SMEs) have significantly increased their activities in South Africa, contributing proportionally to increased employment rates, from 52% to 57% of the GDP (Otache & Usman, 2024). This expansion coincided with government programmes meant to help SMEs in several industries from 1994. The contribution of small company support to the increase of national income implies that efficient financing could directly influence development. Economists counter that household welfare or development at the grassroots level is not always guaranteed by GDP increase (Walker et al., 2021). The poverty rate in South Africa has not dropped proportionately, even with higher business activity. Nevertheless, the Small Enterprise Development Agency (SEDA) has given non-financial support and monitoring to advance business sustainability (Sishuba, 2020). Hence, a longitudinal study is required to improve policies for household development after over two decades. Should economic growth create employment, the proportion of young people facing unemployment should have dropped dramatically.

Although a reported 91% increase post-1994 shows the absolute numerical growth of businesses compared to the mere 8.7% recorded during the apartheid era, a more complex picture is warranted given the potential of focused economic transformation interventions. This numerical change reflects the significant increase in Black business registration brought about by initiatives that offer financial support and development prospects. Still, research indicates that the growth and sustainability of small businesses remain a significant issue in South Africa despite a boost in business development (Rens et al., 2021). This contradiction suggests that the effective running of business enterprises is an ongoing concern, which could explain the high failure rates of the businesses established during the post-apartheid period. In South Africa, more than 50% of the

2.5 million small businesses are in the country. However, the rate of small business failure in South Africa needs to be quantified to understand the magnitude of the problem. The literature shows that about 80% of small businesses in South Africa cannot operate beyond 5 years (Fatoki, 2012; Mbonyane & Ladzani, 2011; SEDA, 2016). About 50% of these small businesses will not survive for 2 years before they fail to remain in operation. Certain sections of the literature emphasised inadequate finance as the problem, while others found regulatory issues, crime rate, and inability to manage business as major challenges among others (Rogerson, 2008; Cant & Wiid, 2013). There is a high possibility that small businesses cannot grow well in South Africa due to the socio-political and economic situation that is largely systemic and historical. Businesses that are easy to start, like retail, have a high failure rate in South Africa, according to a study (Rogerson, 2008). The fundamental issue transcends beyond access to financial resources. It indicates a pressing need for substantially restructuring business management strategies designed to empower Black business owners and promote lasting success. Essentially, entrepreneurs need to be equipped with the know-how and tools to navigate the complexities of running a business successfully.

An enduring legacy of systemic oppression presents a significant obstacle to progress, fostering a pervasive sense of fear and a learned consciousness of dependency, as documented by Du Toit and Neves (2017). Before 1994, the apartheid system systematically suppressed independent thought in Black communities, fostering a culture of fear (Hocoy, 2020) that enforced strict behavioural norms and hindered creative personal development. The emergence of democracy initiated a phase of political liberation; however, a preliminary misunderstanding occurred, conflating political freedom with instant economic equality. The architects of post-apartheid transformation policies did not operate under this flawed assumption. They commenced a series of comprehensive consultations to establish a new South Africa, which involved targeted support for Black entrepreneurship, mainly aimed at empowering historically disadvantaged women. The objective was to tackle the previous system's economic consequences rather than presume that change would occur spontaneously.

If cultural factors represent an obstacle, specialised training programmes should be incorporated into policies to promote small business development in South Africa since successful financial management requires financial literacy, discipline, and accountability. Black-owned enterprises necessitate structural transformation (Bell et al., 2018) to foster sustainable practices in technological advancements and other essential areas. It is essential to prioritise grassroots business development in economically disadvantaged communities, integrating relevant training into all financial support offered to entrepreneurs. Research indicates that the majority of South African business owners (51.5%) seem reluctant to opt for bank financing or consider available borrowing options to grow their business (Kongolo, 2010) despite challenges in raising funds. Hence, it can be deduced that there is an evident gap between perceived needs and available resources, which leads to questioning the relevance of existing traditional financial models compared to the actual difficulties entrepreneurs face. This highlights the potential for small business owners, informed about government financing options, to become excessively dependent on these resources, possibly overlooking the strategic use of credit for operational expansion. Such unawareness underscores the necessity for a comprehensive support strategy that transcends mere financial assistance, emphasising the empowerment of entrepreneurs by providing essential knowledge and skills for sustainable success.

The availability of bank financing, associated interest rates, and overall borrowing costs are a considerable deterrent for numerous potentially viable businesses. The financial burden, along with the stagnation in growth after governmental support, has been identified in the literature as a contributing factor to the high failure rate of businesses post-1994. Many small enterprises forgo credit to finance their operations (Kongolo, 2010). The long-term sustainability of businesses cannot depend exclusively on government-sponsored programmes and funding. It is essential to enhance awareness among business owners about alternative growth strategies, as a strong economy requires the establishment of more extensive, revenue-generating enterprises that can promote employment and contribute to societal development. The objective is to enable entrepreneurs to consider long-term strategies, focusing on developing resilient and self-sufficient businesses that enhance the broader economic environment.

3 Policy Contexts of Post-Apartheid in Small Business Financing

The conceptual framework for post-1994 transformation policies regarding small business and development aims to empower South Africans, particularly Black individuals, who have experienced considerable economic marginalisation due to systemic resource deprivation. It is essential to recognise that 'resources' encompass a multifaceted array of factors, and insufficient financial resources alone do not fully account for the policy deficiencies that hindered economic development prior to liberation (Bushe, 2019). Although financial resources existed in the pre-apartheid era, there is insufficient evidence to indicate that Black-owned businesses would have thrived (Ssekitoleko & du Plessis, 2021). The systematic suppression of economic agency compelled Black individuals into precarious employment within the informal sector, marked by exploitative wages and excessive workloads, with earnings predominantly directed towards basic sustenance. The intentional fostering of economic vulnerability functioned as a strategic approach to sustain intellectual and economic dependency, reinforcing social control. The issue extended beyond mere fund withholding; it systematically eroded economic self-determination.

In this instance, resource waste seems to be linked to human factors rather than inadequate policy implementation or execution. The lasting effects of oppression and the subsequent entrenched cultural norms created within Black-owned businesses are often overlooked in academic literature and policy analysis. This oversight reveals a widespread misconception that readily available financial resources will automatically lead to an immediate and absolute economic transformation and development (Balkaran, 2017). Nevertheless, understanding the intricacies of the historical backdrop of imposed incapacitation within Black communities, particularly regarding business development, remains essential. Such an understanding could profoundly enhance a critical reassessment of the ongoing inefficiencies and constrained effectiveness evident in governmental programmes and interventions aimed at entrepreneurs. In order to effectively confront the challenges we face, it is essential to transcend rudimentary economic frameworks and immerse ourselves in the authentic experiences and historical contexts of the individuals these policies aim to benefit.

The apartheid regime systematically denied Black individuals fundamental rights, including land ownership, company formation, and participation in substantive business activities. The conceptual terminologies of colonialism and apartheid are not the same. Colonialism speaks to the economic and social structure that happened in South Africa before 1910 (Christopher et al., 2002), while apartheid is racial segregation and economic exclusion which occurred between 1948 and 1994, but colonialism, however, projects racial economic control (Seekings, 2008). In the context of this book, post-apartheid economic transformation is based on redressing racial discrimination through operating businesses and benefiting from economic activities. Furthermore, rather than focusing on the training and development of the Black workforce, the system chose to employ Asian labourers in essential sectors like mining (Hetherington, 1994). The transformation policies implemented after 1994 aimed, in part, to address these historical injustices. The primary principle was that achieving economic empowerment for Black South Africans would result in concrete opportunities for business ownership and access to developmental financial assistance. This reformative or positive action involved the ability to acquire and utilise land for economic activities in order to promote job creation. Despite significant advancements in funding policies, an apparent lack of evidence indicates that the conceptual framework has led to a thorough transformation of the mindsets and cultural paradigms that contributed to previous failures (Gardner, 2006). This oversight is particularly troubling, considering the significant number of Black-owned companies that have undergone liquidation due to issues such as corruption, misappropriation of funds, insufficient accountability, and overall mismanagement (Bhorat et al., 2017). These occurrences suggest that the required support extends beyond financial resources, including developing tools necessary for sustainable business management.

Small businesses operating in South African townships are unique in that they are informal and seldom depend on readily available financial resources and regulations put in place. Though their informal nature promotes operational flexibility, this method of operation often highlights limited access to essential funding and crucial knowledge needed for durable sustainability. The lack of information and financial resources disproportionately impacts rural communities, limiting their ability for self-directed development. Policy initiatives must extend beyond financial provision to develop a comprehensive support system that fosters the success of small businesses.

Following the transition to democracy in 1994, many townships have experienced persistently high crime rates and sluggish rural development (Clack & Minnaar, 2018). To address criminality and foster community advancement, initial proposals included funding policies aimed at small business development. Evidence suggests that township financial allocations are frequently underutilised or inaccessible to the intended beneficiaries (Shackleton et al., 2018). This discrepancy highlights a fundamental issue that transcends policy design, underscoring the critical importance of human factors in efficiently allocating resources. Without a comprehensive analysis of the human factors, financial assistance is insufficient for fostering significant change in township economies. Understanding the socio-cultural dynamics, existing skill sets, and prevailing attitudes toward entrepreneurship in these communities is essential to ensure that funds are used optimally.

Although the objectives and anticipated outcomes of post-1994 development policies are clearly defined, a significant gap remains in our comprehension of their acceptance and execution at the community level. Questions specifically pertain to the duration required for township residents, despite receiving specialised business training and understanding of prospects, to utilise money and attain the desired policy objectives successfully. In light of the history of economic marginalisation, the desired outcomes are often unattained, which illustrates that factors impacting business success go beyond the conceptual framework of post-1994 policy actions. The overemphasis on financial assistance without addressing entrenched psychological and cultural systemic oppression may be a contributing element to this imbalance. Decades into democracy, the ever-increasing unemployment rate highlights the inefficiencies of existing policies on sustainable economic growth. This failure exacerbates existing inequities and disparities in budget distribution, creating a new kind of inequality within the post-apartheid setting, presumably arising from the core conceptualisation of the programmes. It prompts us to question whether the human dimension has been sufficiently considered and if a purely financial approach is appropriate to alleviate the enduring effects of oppression.

4 Disparities in Accessing Funding and Credit for Business

An analysis of Lekaba's (2023) findings shows that accessing funding for small businesses remains challenging in South Africa. Although a significant amount of financial resources has been allocated to this sector since 1994, corruption and political agendas heavily influence funding distribution—moreover, complexities in accessing business point to blatant human interferences. Notably, financial institutions apply strict credit record criteria, which puts historically marginalised individuals at a disadvantage. Furthermore, previous beneficiaries of funds who have mishandled said funds face a series of barriers to further credit access. Credit behaviours and financial management extend beyond a mere policy problem; they are deeply rooted in human and cultural contexts, a reality observed across Africa, not solely within South Africa. Conversely, research shows a positive correlation between access to credit and business development, highlighting the potential for financial resources to stimulate growth (Kongolo, 2010). Simultaneously, there is a significant necessity to strengthen the credit system, as an increasing number of small businesses have shown potential for growth through its use in recent years. However, the strict criteria regulating loan eligibility pose a considerable barrier to sectoral growth. Location and provincial GDP levels significantly affect credit access for entrepreneurs, with those in Gauteng, KZN, and the Western Cape having a noticeable advantage. The edge given to these entrepreneurs has resulted in significant growth in these regions, while others remain dependent on informal credit sources (Kongolo, 2010).

While government funding for small businesses is seen as an economic growth factor, its sustainability in post-apartheid South Africa remains questioned. As previously mentioned, location and ease of access to financial institutions directly influence credit allocation, impacting business growth. This imbalance explains the reason for the majority of public support in urban areas, where businesses have greater access to formal credit facilities. Moreover, a general lack of managerial skills is responsible for the high failure rate of most small businesses established after 1994.

Thus, an important question emerges: Had colonial powers created an environment conducive to entrepreneurial growth and progressive ideas within Black communities, what path would their intellectual and economic evolution have taken? Some argue that the capitalist ideologies of White supremacy were developed to instil a sense of economic reliance in Black people, thus trapping them in a vicious cycle of earning and spending. In other words, political independence did not ensure psychological freedom from capitalist ideologies. The status quo even extends to the emerging middle class, who often face financial difficulties and are over-reliant on jobs rather than entrepreneurial activities. This state of affairs is further exacerbated by the exodus of African professionals seeking greener pastures abroad and working in fields unrelated to their academic training. In addition, individuals interested in breaking into the business world often face significant hurdles linked to high interest rates and investors' reluctance. These challenges are intimately intertwined with political dynamics and elitist mindsets, with those in power dominating the less fortunate. Consequently, this lack of opportunity (for both the educated and non-educated) often leads to crimes and further slows business growth in South Africa.

On the other hand, informal financial sources result in limited business growth (Kongolo, 2010). A lack of structured monitoring and sufficient funding from informal sources stifles business growth and negatively influences operation expansion. South Africa continues to face several obstacles in its bid to reach economic inclusivity, especially regarding the distribution of funding resources. Although small business funding policies explicitly emphasise inclusivity, evidence indicates that achieving equitable resource distribution continues to be challenging (Nengomasha, 2021). The South African economy has demonstrated considerable volatility in recent years, marked by varying outputs and a simultaneous reduction of resources allocated for development. Nevertheless, business support programmes are essential for people living in rural communities. The abrupt reduction of these programmes may worsen current unemployment rates, potentially undermining the nation's security framework as competition for limited resources escalates. The issue extends beyond economic factors to encompass social dimensions, necessitating a comprehensive understanding of the effects of economic pressures on community stability and well-being.

4.1 Competition for Resources

Since 1994, the South African government has consistently allocated financial resources to small business development while facing criticism for favouring established, well-resourced industries over sectors considered vital for broader economic growth (Irene, 2017). It is contended that genuine economic development in South Africa requires reallocating resources away from established businesses and sectors. The recent emergence of digital transformation has introduced disruptive forces, presenting a considerable challenge to small enterprises, especially those located in townships or owned by individuals with limited digital proficiency. Thus, the government must urgently respond to the changing global business environment and the transformative effects of technology, incorporating these factors into strategic measures designed to promote growth in critical sectors. In other words, the Broad-Based Black Economic Empowerment (BBBEE) Programme needs to be thoroughly evaluated. The review should go beyond redressing inequalities and adopt a comprehensive approach, highlighting broad-based inclusivity. Data show that government policies are misdirected (see Seekings & Nattrass, 2011), ineffectively addressing issues surrounding poverty, joblessness, and inequality in most cases. The main concern is to determine how to realign policy to recognise and address the misalignment between funding priorities and essential resource needs for sustainable economic development in South Africa.

A further important issue is the concern of effectively and responsibly managing businesses to achieve outcomes corresponding to the allocated resources. Responsible leadership in small businesses and a strong accountability framework are crucial, regardless of the racial or ethnic background of the owners or their participation in government programmes. Nonetheless, despite the significant influx of resources into small business initiatives after 1994, a persistent issue is the evident lack of accountability in allocating these funds. This issue may be partially ascribed to the distinctive complexities of the South African business environment and the intrinsic challenges of operating small enterprises in the post-apartheid context (Ekene & Kelly, 2023).

Allocating, distributing, and utilising public funds remains a significant point of contention among stakeholders. Trade unions and similar entities responsible for protecting the economic interests of South Africa often prioritised their agendas (Schneider & Medina, 2018). Policy formulation has proven to be profoundly political and involves protecting specific interests. This situation, in which personal agendas and interests are prioritised over the national goal of economic growth, results in the less dominant being marginalised and forced to compete for limited resources. Implementing robust policies to ensure the effective allocation of financial resources for small businesses is crucial (Goga et al., 2019). To ensure optimal resource utilisation and achieve intended outcomes, the decision-making process must be fundamentally democratic and devoid of bias or undue human influence.

The premise for prioritising funding to support small businesses in the post-apartheid context lies in creating jobs and economic development (Balkaran, 2017). Nonetheless, financial resources attribution does not directly equate to creating employment opportunities. It is essential to deploy these resources in a way that promotes sustainable economic growth and development. The expansion of businesses generally creates opportunities for enhanced employment, which can subsequently drive business growth from small-scale operations to larger, more significant enterprises. This indicates the possibilities for significant economic transformation by focused funding for small businesses. However, the current situation often differs from the expected potential and is marked by frequent inefficient fund utilisation. Effective strategies require incorporating thorough training programmes and strong monitoring systems within small business support policies, ensuring the efficient use of allocated funds. In efforts to engender rapid economic transformation, the government has underestimated the deeply entrenched systemic issues and various human factors affecting the successful implementation of small business funding initiatives.

4.2 Human Capital Development in Small Business Financing

Discussions on corporate financing require a rigorous assessment of Human Capital Development (HDI). According to UNDP (2022), the Human Development Index could mean or may be used to measure figures related to education, income, and life expectancy. In the context of South Africa, assessment of capital development is how individual business owners' education, for instance, is used to generate income and consequently leads to social progress. The importance of HDI is highlighted in education transformation and its application as a governmental intervention for the advancement of small business owners (Gamede & Uleanya, 2017). The observed slump in business growth and the continued failure of small businesses result from lacking human capital capacity. Fundamental components for promoting business sustainability include fundamental education and specialised training in business management. Hence, access to quality education is prioritised in the transformation agenda of 1998 in a post-apartheid era. The underlying principle is that government funding and support for post-secondary education would grant access to primarily Black Africans, especially women, to receive education and training for personal growth. The skills acquired from these educational courses were expected to equip graduates with entrepreneurial skills. However, the continuous rise in graduate unemployment rates and graduates working in unrelated fields indicates a potential misalignment between educational outcomes (supply) and labour market demands. This calls for a funding shift, emphasising training that directly equips young people with business and job-creation skills to combat poverty. Human capital development must be rethought in light of South Africa's transformation agenda.

Supporting HDI could also mean economic transformation by supporting young people, including women. This is underpinned by the idea of youth social transformation in post-apartheid South Africa (see Odeku, 2019). The significant youth population in South Africa necessitates their active involvement in economic development. Young people require access to quality education and targeted training, coupled with opportunities for meaningful economic engagement, to divert their energies from unproductive and potentially destructive activities, such as criminal behaviour.

A demonstrable correlation exists between the prevalence of youth-owned businesses and positive economic outcomes, including a reduction in crime rates. Conversely, rising unemployment rates and disengagement from youth-oriented business support policies are likely to exacerbate crime levels, particularly among young men. Therefore, a funding approach that overly prioritises women's businesses and disregards the economic engagement of young men constitutes a threat to crime reduction efforts.

The current discussion on governmental involvement and its critiques highlights local government's essential function in reshaping the narrative of policy shortcomings. The Black African youth residing in townships critically emphasise local governance engagement. These youth, often lacking critical skills for strategic planning and career progression, necessitate targeted interventions to enhance their development. Business development initiatives should include collaborations between local governments and the private sector to create programmes promoting youth entrepreneurship and job creation in these areas.

Concerns are raised over ineffective management strategies in rural areas due to funds misappropriation and lack of public funding. Consequently, re-evaluating individuals responsible for promoting and developing the rural community is essential. A distinct correlation exists between the level of economic development efforts in rural areas and the corresponding crime rates in those regions. Existing literature reveals low local government performance, implying potential neglect of vital economic development efforts aimed at youth, women, and their communities. The efforts of local governments to ensure the economic development of the youthful population, particularly women, are important. Literature has shown a critical skill shortage in rural communities, largely due to problems of resources and governance issues (Nel & Rogerson, 2016). It appears that local government failures to see youth and women as important resources for local government development are also linked to poor performance of municipalities (Rogerson, 2018; Mbanga & Tsenoli, 2013). Possible reasons for this occurrence are a lack of comprehension of national policies or exclusionary frameworks that fail to address the needs of particular populations effectively. The post-apartheid era has witnessed significant corporate expansion, propelled mainly by various intervention strategies concentrated in urban regions. Nonetheless, these advancements have mostly failed to benefit rural communities.

4.3 Gender Factor

A critical aspect of the government's transformation agenda is its ability to empower women-owned businesses. Research has continuously underlined women's historical marginalisation preceding the formal apartheid frameworks. While legislation promoting discrimination against women played a role in the status quo, the leading causes of this discrimination are deeply entrenched in socio-cultural norms, subjugating women to men historically. These systems typically stressed familial obligations over professional prospects, a mentality regrettably endures in numerous

South African cultural contexts, even in the post-apartheid period. Consequently, the impetus for transformative policies aimed at advancing women entrepreneurs and their enterprises extends beyond merely addressing the legacy of apartheid. These transformation programmes acknowledge the unyielding influence of deep-rooted, culturally ingrained prejudices within some Black African groups. Thus, a prudent shift to enhance women's active involvement in business activities while preserving an inclusive framework for all groups is essential within the scope of comprehensive reform initiatives.

Fourie (2017) examined the intricacies of South Africa's economic transition following apartheid, emphasising the government's goal of fostering job creation in the private sector. The government's significant control over resource allocation undeniably influences the economy's trajectory. Post-apartheid economic transformation analyses often intersect with inequality studies, especially regarding gender disparities. The fundamental assertion is that the governing authority is accountable for the outcomes of its policies, whether deliberate or inadvertent, encompassing the fair allocation of resources among genders. Conversely, government officials often defend resource allocation strategies, stressing their well-intentioned aims. There is a dominant perception among citizens that systemic corruption exists within political circles, linking ongoing racial and gender inequalities to this misconduct despite three decades of democratic governance. In other words, this sentiment indicates that South Africans are facing a novel type of economic inequality, comparable to an 'economic apartheid', arising from the perceived unfair allocation of resources. One would argue that policies ought to restrict corruption and ensure the effective allocation of resources to promote economic development. Recent trends indicate that policies have been disregarded or manipulated for the personal gains of those in charge of resource distribution. Thus, genuine economic prosperity and transformation depend upon a significant change in the mindset of policymakers and public finance leaders. Three decades into democracy, issues of escalating poverty, elevated unemployment rates, and persistent criminality persist, which highlights the urgent need for an exhaustive re-evaluation of transformative policies, particularly about rural development methods.

5 Agricultural Business Development as a Solution

Agricultural business development presents a significant opportunity for equitable economic growth, particularly in traditionally marginalised rural regions. Effective policies are anticipated to prioritise funding and support for agricultural and rural business projects. Rigorous monitoring is essential to ensure that the growth of the agricultural sector directly benefits Black South Africans. Post-apartheid literature on this issue demonstrates that Black individuals are often reduced to working in low-wage agricultural employment, such as labourers and fruit pickers, thus further growing economic benefits for the White minority. Indeed, while Black people contribute to food security for the country, this contribution does not yield commensurate economic emancipation.

Governmental interventions should have included substantial investments in mechanised farming infrastructure in rural communities, specifically for Black-owned farms. Such ventures would promote business growth, employment opportunities, and rural development. A notable mismatch exists in agricultural education and commercial development in South Africa and the rest of the continent. This is further demonstrated by an increased emphasis on food security, which reveals the importance of agriculture in economic sustainability. Hence, calls for governmental acts emphasising agriculture are justified, as agriculture ensures food security and a healthy population and is vital for African development. Developing the agricultural sector requires collaboration among ministers of different portfolios to encourage agricultural studies among youth. Policies must deliberately position agriculture as a crucial driver for poverty alleviation and unemployment reduction. This could enhance South Africa's competitive advantage in global markets by leveraging agricultural products to boost national income and improve exchange rates. Historically, official support has often been directed towards regions that have yielded negligible developmental results. However, it is imperative to acknowledge that these assertions require significant empirical evidence.

6 Datasets

This study draws upon extensive data from the Adult Population Survey (APS) administered to 2000 adults in Global Entrepreneurship Monitor (GEM) countries, including South Africa. The survey collected key information regarding entrepreneurial activities, attitudes, and aspirations. The collection is particularly noteworthy as it contains specific information regarding entrepreneurial characteristics, including the motivations and ambitions that drive individuals to establish businesses. These indicators are meticulously aligned with the central focus of this book. Since 1994, a persistent narrative in South Africa has been on the challenges faced by entrepreneurs, particularly emphasising the perceived lack of capital access as a primary reason leading to business failure, especially among certain demographic groups. As such, the APS dataset offers a unique opportunity to move beyond anecdotal evidence and examine the behavioural patterns influencing entrepreneurial actions. Examining these trends facilitates a more refined understanding of how such activities may have impacted the success or failure of businesses established in the post-apartheid era.

The indicators used to demonstrate the couple nature of entrepreneurial activity include perceived opportunities rate, perceived capabilities rate, fear of failure rate, entrepreneurial intentions rate, Total early-stage Entrepreneurial Activity (TEA) rate, Established Business Ownership Rate, Entrepreneurial Employee Activity rate, Entrepreneurial Employee Activity rate, Motivational Index, Female/Male TEA ratio, Female/Male Opportunity-Driven TEA ratio, High Job Creation Expectation Rate, Innovation Rate, Business Services Sector rate, High Status to Successful Entrepreneurs rate, and Entrepreneurship as a Good Career Choice rate. However, this book focuses explicitly on variables related to gender dynamics, entrepreneurial activities, and the primary motivations of business owners. The study employed the Entrepreneurial Framework Conditions (EFCs) and pertinent indicators to analyse the detected trends in the data. This methodological choice ensured that the findings were grounded in a solid theoretical framework, facilitating a more nuanced and insightful examination of the data.

Likewise, the book uses an entrepreneurial behaviour and attitudes dataset (Source: https://www.gemconsortium.org/wiki/1154).

The company collects data on entrepreneurial characteristics, including motivations and ambitions for starting a business. These indicators are fundamentally important and relevant to the focus of this book. Since 1994, the argument regarding why businesses fail has primarily been related to funding or the inaccessibility of funds to certain demographics. This data will assist in understanding the behavioural aspects of starting a business and how these may affect the success of businesses established after 1994. The company administered the Adult Population Survey (APS) to 2000 adults in GEM countries, including South Africa. The survey collected entrepreneurial activity, attitudes, and aspirations.

- **Perceived Opportunities Rate**: Percentage of 18–64 population (individuals involved in any stage of entrepreneurial activity excluded) who see good opportunities to start a firm in the area where they live.
- **Perceived Capabilities Rate**: Percentage of 18–64 population (individuals involved in any stage of entrepreneurial activity excluded) who believe they have the required skills and knowledge to start a business.
- **Fear of Failure Rate:** Percentage of 18–64 population (individuals involved in any stage of entrepreneurial activity excluded) who indicate that fear of failure would prevent them from setting up a business.
- **Entrepreneurial Intentions Rate**: Percentage of 18–64 population (individuals involved in any stage of entrepreneurial activity excluded) who are latent entrepreneurs and who intend to start a business within three years.
- **Total early-stage Entrepreneurial Activity (TEA) Rate**: Percentage of 18–64 population who are either nascent entrepreneurs or owner-managers of a new business.
- **Established Business Ownership Rate**: Percentage of 18–64 population who are currently an owner-manager of an established business, i.e., owning and managing a running business that has paid salaries, wages, or any other payments to the owners for more than 42 months.
- **Entrepreneurial Employee Activity Rate**: Rate of involvement of employees in entrepreneurial activities, such as developing or launching new goods or services, or setting up a new business unit, a new establishment, or a subsidiary.

- **Motivational Index**: Percentage of those involved in TEA who are improvement-driven opportunity motivated, divided by the percentage of TEA that is necessity-motivated.
- **Female/Male TEA Ratio**: Percentage of female 18–64 population who are either nascent entrepreneurs or owner-managers of a 'new business', divided by the equivalent percentage for their male counterparts.
- **Female/Male Opportunity-Driven TEA Ratio**: Percentage of those females involved in TEA who (i) claim to be driven by opportunity as opposed to finding no other option for work; and (ii) who indicate the main driver for being involved in this opportunity is being independent or increasing their income, rather than just maintaining their income, divided by the equivalent percentage for their male counterparts.
- **High Job Creation Expectation Rate**: Percentage of those involved in TEA who expect to create six or more jobs in 5 years.
- **Innovation Rate**: Percentage of those involved in TEA who indicate that their product or service is new to at least some customers AND that few/no businesses offer the same product.
- **Business Services Sector Rate**: Percentage of those involved in TEA in the 'Business Services' sector—Information and Communication, Financial Intermediation and Real Estate, Professional Services or Administrative Services, as defined by the ISIC 4.0 Business Type Codebook.
- **High Status to Successful Entrepreneurs Rate**: Percentage of 18–64 population who agree that successful entrepreneurs receive high status in their country.
- **Entrepreneurship as a Good Career Choice Rate**: Percentage of 18–64 population who agree that most people consider starting a business as a desirable career choice in their country.

The indicators includes perceived opportunities rate, perceived capabilities rate, fear of failure rate, entrepreneurial intensions rate, Total early-stage Entrepreneurial Activity (TEA) Rate, Established Business Ownership Rate, Entrepreneurial Employee Activity Rate, Entrepreneurial Employee Activity Rate, Motivational Index, Female/Male TEA Ratio, Female/

Male Opportunity-Driven TEA Ratio, High Job Creation Expectation Rate, Innovation Rate, Business Services Sector Rate, Business Services Sector Rate, High Status to Successful Entrepreneurs Rate, and Entrepreneurship as a Good Career Choice Rate. However, only aspects related to gender, entrepreneurial activities and motivation of business owners were analysed for the purpose of this book publication. The idea is to show trends over time.

- **Entrepreneurial Framework Conditions (EFCs):** The nine conditions identified by GEM that enhance (or hinder) new business creation in a given country, and provide the basis of the NES.
- **Entrepreneurial Finance**: The availability of financial resources—equity and debt—for small and medium enterprises (SMEs) (including grants and subsidies).
- **Governmental Policies: Support and Relevance**: The extent to which public policies support entrepreneurship—entrepreneurship as a relevant economic issue.
- **Government Policies: Taxes and Bureaucracy**: The extent to which public policies support entrepreneurship—taxes or regulations are either size-neutral or encourage new and SMEs.
- **Government Entrepreneurship Programmes**: The presence and quality of programmes directly assisting SMEs at all levels of government (national, regional, municipal).

In relation to Entrepreneurial Framework Conditions (EFCs), the indicators include Entrepreneurial Finance in terms of financial resources availability and access to finance for SMEs in South Africa. Another indicator is Governmental Policies in terms of support and relevance for entrepreneurial activities, and relevance to the economics of South Africa, for instance. Likewise, another indicator is Government Policies in relation to taxes and bureaucracy. This measures whether taxes, for instance, encourage SME activities in the country.

The Government Entrepreneurship Programmes indicator seeks to understand the existence of government programmes for SME owners at all levels of government and their quality.

The Entrepreneurial Education at the school stage indicator determines whether schooling encourages entrepreneurial training at the primary and secondary levels.

- **Entrepreneurial Education at School Stage**: The extent to which training in creating or managing SMEs is incorporated within the education and training system at primary and secondary levels.
- **Entrepreneurial Education at Post School Stage**: The extent to which training in creating or managing SMEs is incorporated within the education and training system in higher education such as vocational, college, business schools, etc.
- **R&D Transfer**: The extent to which national research and development will lead to new commercial opportunities and is available to SMEs.

Similarly, the Entrepreneurial Education at the post-school stage indicator includes higher education and other higher education institutions.

The Research and Development transfer indicator measures the extent to which national research and development can provide opportunities for SMEs.

Other indicators include commercial and legal infrastructure, such as the presence of property rights and other legal assistance to support the activities of SMEs.

The internal market dynamics indicator measures the level of change in the market from year to year. While, the internal market burdens or entry regulation indicator measures the extent to which new firms are free to enter existing markets.

The physical infrastructure indicator looks at ease of access to physical resources such as communication, utilities, transportation, land, or space at a price that does not discriminate against SMEs.

Lastly, the Cultural and Social Norms indicator measures the extent to which social and cultural norms encourage new business or increase wealth and income.

This book uses the National Expert Survey (NES) collected by the company. The NES is administered to 36 'experts' in each GEM country and collects data on the context in which entrepreneurship takes place in a country.

- **Commercial and Legal Infrastructure**: The presence of property rights, commercial, accounting, and other legal and assessment services and institutions that support or promote SMEs.
- **Internal Market Dynamics**: The level of change in markets from year to year.
- **Internal Market Burdens or Entry Regulation**: The extent to which new firms are free to enter existing markets.
- **Physical Infrastructure**: Ease of access to physical resources—communication, utilities, transportation, land, or space—at a price that does not discriminate against SMEs.
- **Cultural and Social Norms**: The extent to which social and cultural norms encourage or allow actions leading to new business methods or activities that can potentially increase personal wealth and income.

Global Entrepreneurship Research Association (GERA): GERA is the umbrella organisation that owns GEM, registered as a private limited not-for-profit company in the United Kingdom. It is funded by National Team fees and the contributions of sponsoring institutions.

Individual-Level Data: A.sav data file, either APS or NES, containing all information for all interviews conducted.

National Expert Survey (NES): The NES is administered to 36 'experts' in each GEM country and collects data on the context in which entrepreneurship takes place in a country. It provides information about the nine aspects of a country's socio-economic milieu that are believed to impact national entrepreneurship significantly—the Entrepreneurship Framework Conditions (EFCs).

National-Level Data: A.sav data file, either APS or NES, containing GEM-calculated rates for an economy or economies.

National Team: GEM is formed of a 'National Teams' consortium. A local university or academic institution leads each team. The team is the official national representative of the project, responsible for collecting GEM data in the country on an annual basis, producing a 'National Report' on their findings, and acting as the point of contact for GEM enquiries.

Request For Proposal (RFP) Package: The package, usually a.zip file, includes all the documents that National Teams need to submit to request approval for data collection and the documents they will need to conduct the surveys.

Request For Proposal (RFP): This is a.pdf document issued by GEM, outlining the requirements for completing the APS and NES in a particular year. It is contained within the RFP package (see above).

Total early-stage Entrepreneurial Activity (TEA): GEM's most well-known index, representing the percentage of the 18–64 population who are either nascent entrepreneurs or owner-managers of a new business.

6.1 South African Governmental Programmes

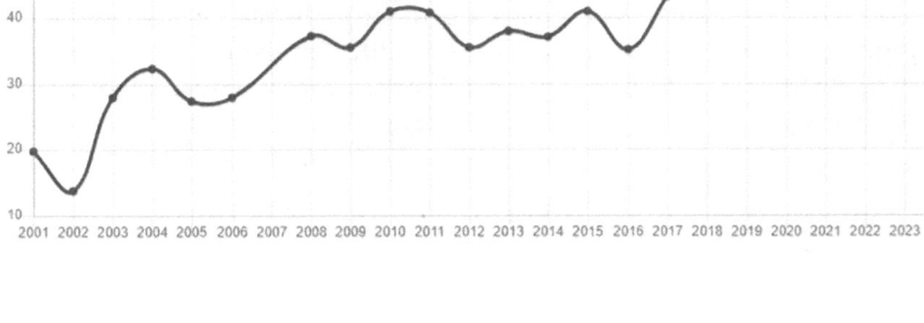

This aspect examines the trends in South African government programmes and initiatives intended to benefit or promote SME activities. A significant finding is a sharp decline in government programmes for SMEs between 2022 and 2023. Over the longer term, from 2001 to 2023, there is no consistent evidence of regular government programmes for business owners. Instead, government support for business owners appears to have peaked only in 2005, 2014, and 2022, with substantial variation in the level of support across these peak periods.

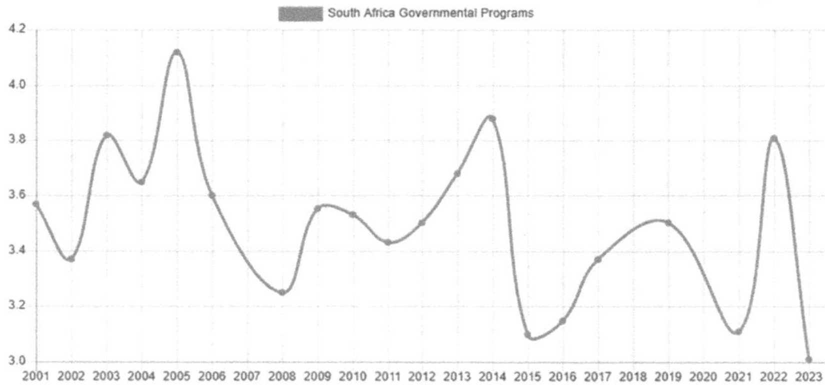

6.2 *South African Financing for Entrepreneurs*

The literature suggests that the availability and accessibility of finance for business growth in the country are limited. The trend analysis supports this, revealing a poor financing trajectory for entrepreneurs. A sharp decline occurred between 2001 and 2002, and SME financing has never recovered to its 2001 level. Subsequent growth has been marginal or insignificant. Notably, financing levels in 2021 mirrored the sharp drop experienced in 2002. This pattern reinforces the literature highlighting the challenges entrepreneurs face in accessing finance within the country.

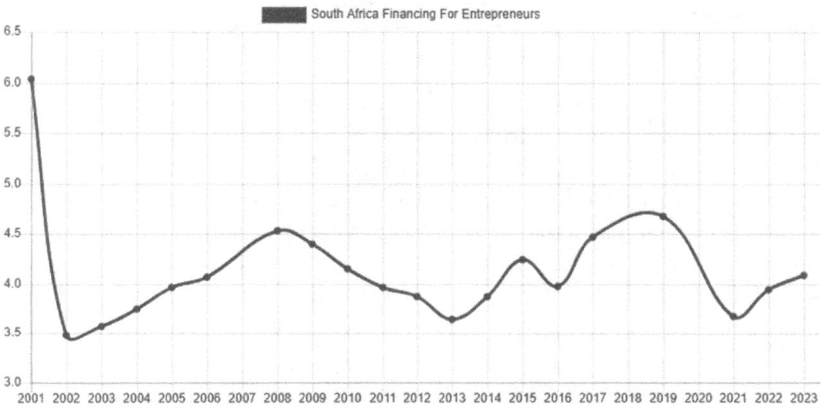

6.3 *South African Governmental Support and Policies*

The chart indicates a sharp decline in government support since 2005, reaching near its lowest point in 2023. This trend highlights a critical need for the government to bolster its support for SMEs and ensure that policies actively promote business activities nationwide. This finding also corroborates previous observations regarding SME financing, as these two aspects are interconnected. In conclusion, a key area of support needed by entrepreneurs is finance, and its continuous decline suggests a persistent lack of adequate support and ineffective policies in addressing this crucial requirement.

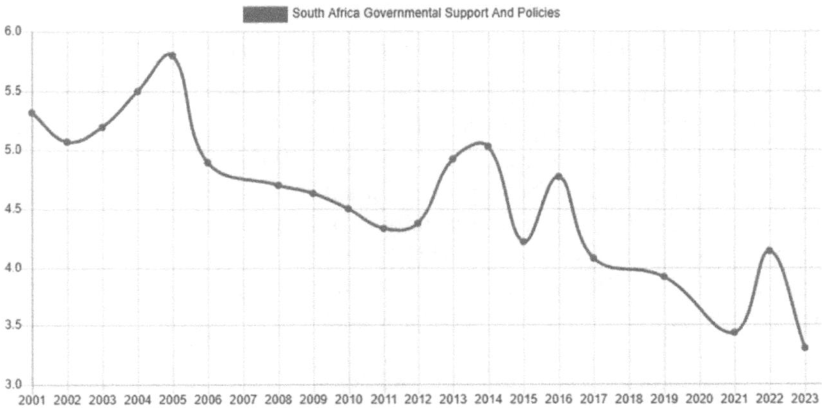

6.4 *South Africa's Internal Market Dynamics and Internal Market Openness*

This section examines the ease of market entry for new entrepreneurs and the level of growth within the South African SME sector. The data presents seemingly contradictory findings. Market entry appears to have become increasingly difficult from 2017 to 2023, with limited evidence of growth potential, particularly after 2022. This trend aligns with previously identified challenges related to inaccessible finance and limited opportunities for business expansion. However, the rate of change indicates a different dynamic, suggesting a significant level of growth specifically from 2021 to 2023.

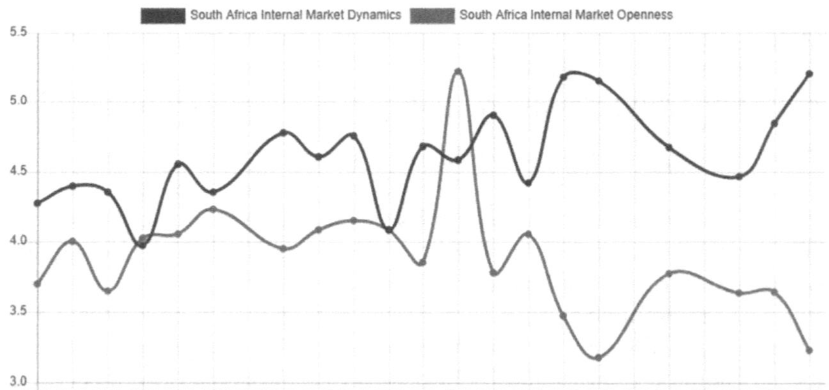

6.5 *South Africa's Physical and Service Infrastructure*

The growth of both physical and services infrastructure reached its lowest point in 2023. This sharp decline began in 2015 and worsened significantly after 2022, coinciding with South Africa's first election after 30 years of democracy. This represents a substantial downturn, the most severe since 2002. It indicates a failure of physical and service infrastructure to effectively support SME activities even six years into the democratic era, a situation that did not improve significantly until 2015 before entering its current downward trajectory.

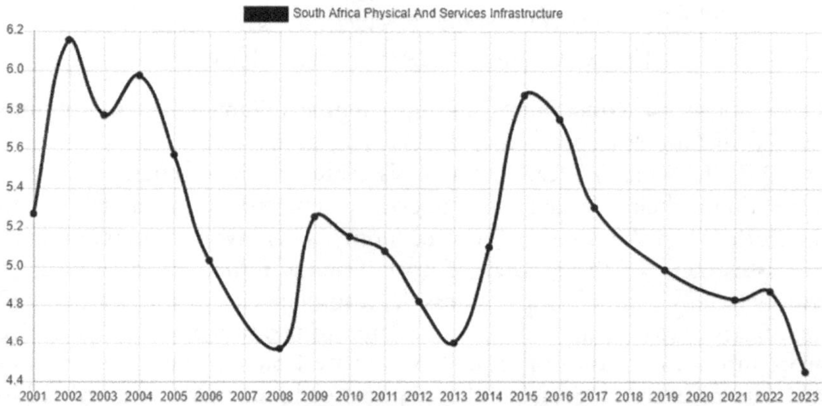

6.6 South African Taxes and Bureaucracy

While the trend of using taxes to support SMEs has been inconsistent, there was a notable, steady upward growth from 2019 to 2022. This increase could be attributed to support packages implemented to assist entrepreneurial activities during the COVID-19 pandemic. A key aim of these measures was likely to simplify bureaucratic processes to provide easier support for small business owners during that challenging period.

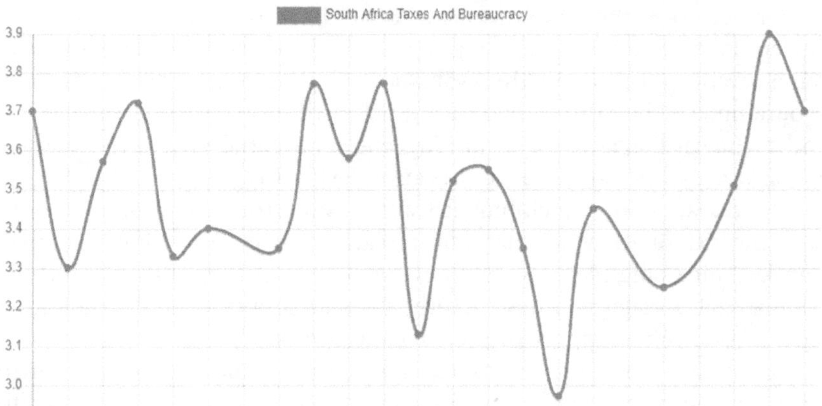

7 Analysis of Entrepreneurial Framework Conditions (EFCs)

The indicators concerning Entrepreneurial Framework Conditions (EFCs) include entrepreneurial finance availability and access to finances for SMEs in South Africa. The analysis evaluated governmental policies, determining their relevance and support for entrepreneurial activities and their effects on the South African economy. This involved a comprehensive assessment of the efficacy of governmental initiatives in fostering a conducive environment for business development. The research examined the effects of governmental policies related to taxation and administrative procedures. This indicator aimed to evaluate how current tax structures and administrative processes either support or hinder SME activity within the country.

Moreover, the existence and effectiveness of government entrepreneurial programmes were examined. This indicator seeks to understand the efficacy of government initiatives at various levels in assisting SME owners by providing critical resources and guidance.

Another indicator is entrepreneurial education at the school stage. In other words, it measures whether schooling encourages entrepreneurial training at primary and secondary levels.

Furthermore, the study also investigated the substantial influence of entrepreneurial education alongside the previously discussed tax and bureaucratic policies and the evaluation of government entrepreneurial programmes. The efficacy of educational institutions, such as universities and technical colleges, in promoting entrepreneurial skills and mindsets across both school and higher education levels was determined.

The research and development transfer indicator was assessed to evaluate the extent to which national research and development initiatives translate into tangible opportunities for SMEs. Other indicators include commercial and legal infrastructure, such as property rights and other legal assistance to support the activities of SMEs.

In addition, the internal market dynamics indicator was employed to evaluate annual market fluctuations since market volatility can significantly impact the viability of SMEs. Internal market burdens and entry regulations were examined to determine the accessibility for new firms in established markets and identify potential barriers to entry that could hinder entrepreneurial activity.

The physical infrastructure indicator looked at ease of access to physical resources such as communication networks, utilities, transportation, and affordable land or space to guarantee that SMEs are not disadvantaged.

Lastly, the inclusion of the cultural and social norms indicator aims to assess the influence of societal attitudes and values on entrepreneurial activities. This indicator assessed the degree to which cultural norms facilitate business creation and wealth generation, emphasising the significant role of social acceptance in fostering a strong entrepreneurial ecosystem.

7.1 South African SMEs Perceived Opportunities

The study examines SME and business owners' perceptions of entrepreneurial opportunities, analysing the evolution of these views from 2001 to 2023, as illustrated in Fig. 1. The data indicates a fluctuating but generally positive trend in perceived opportunity growth from 2001 to 2015. Relative stability was observed from 2016 to 2019.

2019, the year of the COVID-19 pandemic outbreak, saw a moderate decrease in SMEs' perceived access to supportive opportunities, which continued until 2021. Fortunately, a recovery in perceived access to support was observed from 2022 to 2023. The support for SMEs during the COVID-19 pandemic is worth exploring in the context of policy. South Africa is one of the countries that has responded with mechanisms to support small businesses in distress during this period. The support

Fig. 1 Perception of SMEs owners regarding opportunities (2001 to 2023)

includes COVID-19 SME funds (National Treasury, 2020) and the COVID-19 SME debt relief finance scheme (Department of Small Business Development, 2020), among others. The ideas of policy and these supports are to provide relief and ensure continuous economic activities during the pandemic. The sustainability of small businesses is important for the South African government, and it is cited as part of the reason for the support. After COVID-19, the expectation is that these businesses that benefit from this support will continue operating and should make an impact in their communities. While the policies are clear about the purpose of support and expected impact, the recent development about the rate of business failure, unemployment, and crime suggests policy reviews and evaluation of COVID-19 intervention programmes.

These observations lead to an inquiry concerning the equitable distribution of financial opportunities in South Africa. Hence, an examination of how effectively social grants and small business financing initiatives have addressed poverty challenges is required. These findings require re-evaluating and possibly restructuring the strategies used to allocate social grants across different sectors.

7.2 South African Governmental Programmes

The analysis examines trends concerning the South African government's provision of programmes and initiatives that could benefit or promote SME activity. A notable observation is a significant reduction in government SME programmes recorded from 2022 to 2023, as illustrated in Fig. 2. The data reveals a lack of consistent, sustained government programme delivery from 2001 to 2023. Peaks in programme provision were observed exclusively in 2005, 2014, and 2022, exhibiting considerable variation in their magnitude.

Effective government programmes require a comprehensive sectoral analysis to identify economic areas with the potential to promote broader development. As Smith (2022) noted, the uneven development in post-apartheid South Africa highlights the inherent challenges in this process. A contributing factor is the inclination to prioritise sectors that are either saturated or demonstrate limited potential for local and national economic growth.

Moreover, the inequitable resource allocation in various sectors has engendered a new form of inequality, which affects business owners and beneficiaries in Black communities. Therefore, transformation in the

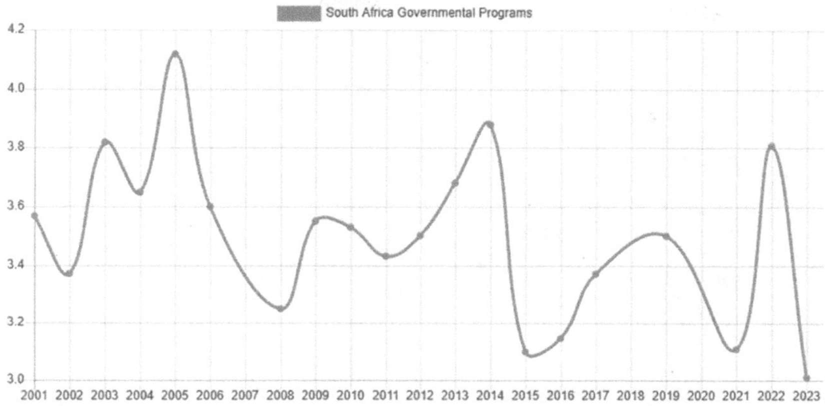

Fig. 2 Government programmes to support SMEs (2001 to 2023)

recent decade must be redefined, focusing on strategic sectorial prioritisation in funding businesses and development programmes. This standpoint is similar to Vivek's (2024) notion of 'transformation deferred', which is based on an analysis of South Africa's development after 1994.

7.3 South African Financing for Entrepreneurs

Research consistently highlights the challenge of limited financial resources and accessibility for entrepreneurs seeking to expand their businesses in South Africa. The data presented substantiates this concern, revealing a trend of inadequate financing for SMEs. A notable decrease occurred from 2001 to 2002, and subsequent recovery initiatives have failed to restore financing levels to those seen in 2001. Minimal and often insignificant increases have marked the growth rate observed post-2002. Interestingly, the considerable decrease observed in 2021 mirrors the prior decline recorded in 2002, highlighting the established difficulties related to entrepreneurial financing in the country. Findings indicate the need to remodel financial strategies and conduct a sectorial analysis of small business development in South Africa. These findings emphasise the inadequacies of interventions that are narrowly focused on benefiting specific, powerful groups, which perpetuates the sustained poverty of marginalised communities.

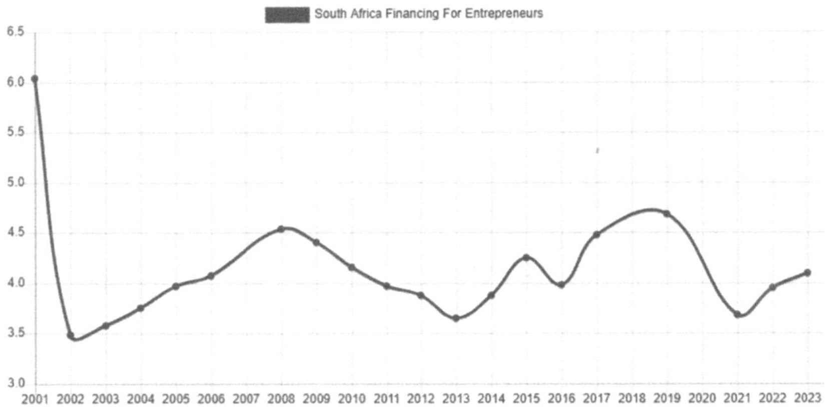

Fig. 3 Trends in financing SMEs in South Africa (2001 to 2023)

The long-running gap between rich and poor in South Africa can be attributed to the constant labour market exploitation and the high rise of capitalism since 1994. It is plausible to anticipate that well-designed interventions will increase economic growth and improve social welfare. Conversely, South Africa has experienced a rise in protests, violence, and multiple crises, mainly due to a continuous lack of opportunities in critical economic sectors (Fig. 3).

7.4 South African Governmental Support and Policies

Figure 4 illustrates an important and continuous decline in governmental support since 2005, leading to an all-time low in 2023. This finding shows the necessity for the government to provide reliable support for SMEs and ensure that policies promote business activities in the country. Moreover, this result speaks to previous findings about issues in SME financing. Therefore, it can be deduced that these concerns are interconnected and that financial support for entrepreneurs is chiefly anticipated. In addition, the continuous decline in governmental support indicates a significant deficiency in existing policies.

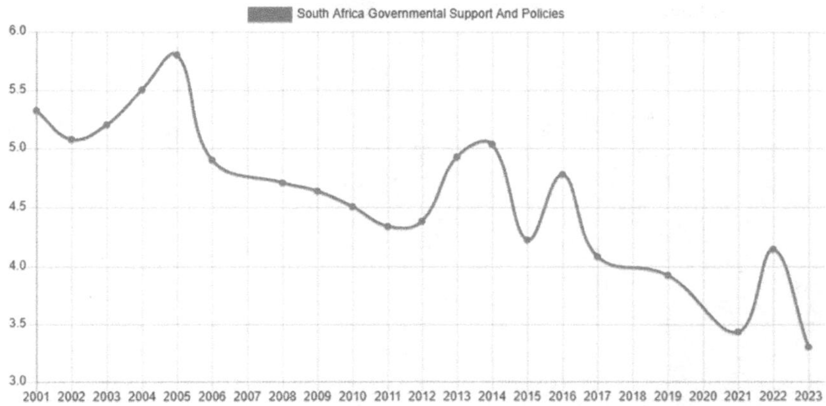

Fig. 4 Governmental supports and policies for SMEs (2001 to 2023)

7.5 *South Africa's Internal Market Dynamics and Internal Market Openness*

This section looks at the market entry dynamics for new entrepreneurs, particularly emphasising the perceived ease of entry and growth potential. The data indicates a significant trend: an observable rise in the challenges associated with entering the SME sector in South Africa from 2017 to 2023. There is a notable absence of evidence suggesting substantial growth opportunities, especially post-2022. This finding underscores the previously recognised challenges associated with restricted access to financing and other resources critical for business expansion (Fig. 5).

An analysis of market dynamics, particularly the degree of change, offers a differing viewpoint. Data showcases the possibility for growth, with significant growth levels from 2021 to 2023. The impact of globalisation and neoliberalism on market dynamics cannot be ignored since global interconnectedness boosted by technological advancements facilitates the swift exchange of skills and goods across national borders. This context prompts an essential inquiry: Who benefits from the market economy and globalisation ideologies?

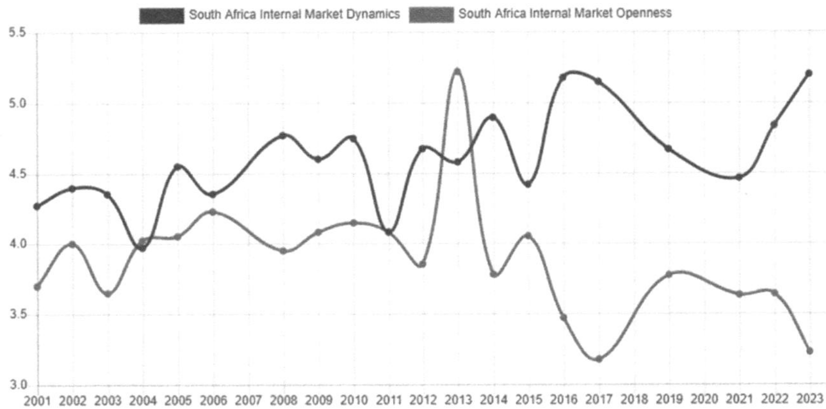

Fig. 5 Levels of growth and ease of market entry as new SMEs (2001 to 2023)

7.6 *South Africa's Physical and Service Infrastructure*

Figure 6 demonstrates a significant reduction in physical and service infrastructure development, culminating in its lowest point in 2023. The significant decline, initiated in 2015, accelerated markedly post-2022, reaching its nadir since 2002, coinciding with South Africa's latest general election, which marks three decades of democratic governance.

The results show that physical and service infrastructures have been continuously inadequate in providing support for SME activities, a pattern that arose 6 years after democracy and which has worsened since 2015. This pattern depicts a form of inequality and marginalisation in terms of resource allocation and access to physical and service infrastructures.

Several South African social movements have associated current affairs with capitalist and neoliberal business practices. Indeed, cheap labour obtained from bordering African nations may have been deemed to be the main reason for this trend. In other words, large enterprises are considered to accumulate profits and wealth at the expense of the well-being of South African citizens. As a result, disposable incomes remain stagnant, while poverty persists despite the increase of local and foreign business enterprises in the country.

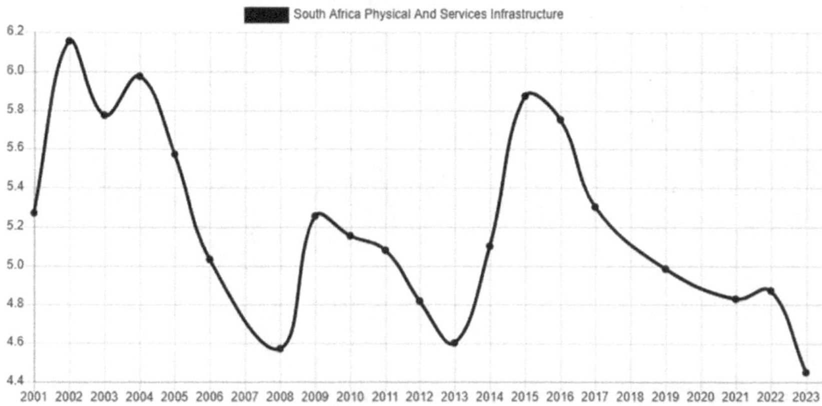

Fig. 6 The growth of physical and services infrastructure for SMEs (2001 to 2023)

7.7 South African Taxes and Bureaucracy

The application of tax measures to support SME activity has shown inconsistency; nonetheless, a significant and sustained upward trend is evident from 2019 to 2022. This positive trend is likely attributable to the implementation of targeted support packages designed to alleviate the economic effects of the COVID-19 pandemic on entrepreneurial activities.

This finding raises a critical inquiry: How can the South African government safeguard, empower, and sustain local enterprises to promote economic development? Sebake (2017) argued for economic policy and interventions about resource control. This concept focuses on the formulation and execution of policies designed to mitigate the exploitation of natural and human resources in sectors deemed essential for South Africa's economic development. As such, the cautious allocation of tax funds is primordial in reaching economic sustainability (Fig. 7).

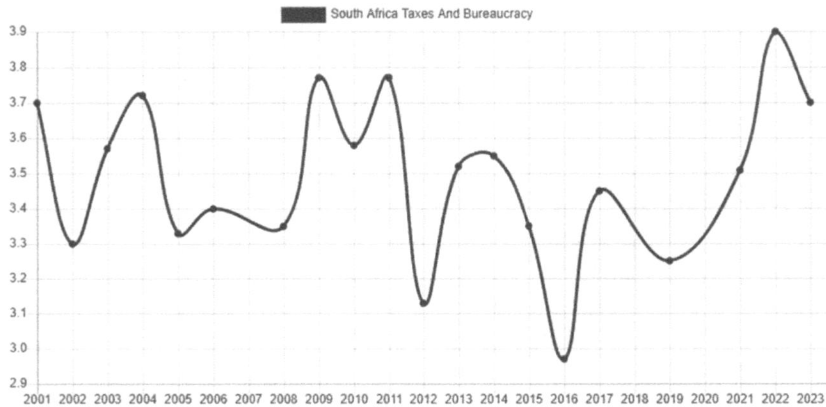

Fig. 7 The trend in using taxes to support SMEs (2001 to 2023)

8 Organisation of Chapters

8.1 Background

This book analyses the effectiveness of Small Business Support programmes in South Africa, tackling enduring challenges and essential concerns associated with market failures. This examination posits that intervention programmes, notwithstanding their well-meaning nature, often fail to yield quantifiable positive outcomes in economic development. This volume articulates and examines theoretical and conceptual frameworks for evaluating the efficacy of state grant-funded initiatives in South Africa.

Theoretical and conceptual frameworks serve as essential tools for assessing the efficacy of government programmes, among various other considerations. The frameworks aim to provide insightful guidance for state programmes in recalibrating their perspectives and objectives, highlighting the significance of implementation, evaluation, and performance in their endeavours.

Moreover, the book is a valuable reference for a diverse array of stakeholders, encompassing development finance institutions (DFIs), multinational entities, and private-sector investors. It comprehensively examines effective methodologies for monitoring, evaluating, and reporting investment programmes, particularly within developing economies. Furthermore, the book aims to provide a pragmatic and theoretically grounded structure for enhancing the efficacy and accountability of support initiatives within challenging economic environments.

8.2 Chapters

Chapter One provides a comprehensive analysis of the various small business support programmes established in South Africa after the conclusion of apartheid. This chapter evaluates the effectiveness of small business assistance programmes, which are crucial for reducing income inequality, generating employment, and fostering economic growth. The evaluation in this chapter aims to determine whether funding initiatives have successfully achieved their pre-set objectives and whether these align with SMEs' expectations. Moreover, implementation challenges are also investigated to identify the underlying reasons for performance disparities, as these challenges and their impact on programme efficacy offer essential insights for guiding future research. The chapter concludes by recommending a thorough evaluation of existing policies.

Chapter Two argues the essential connection between the effectiveness of internal grant approval processes and SMEs' resulting success or revenue generation. The distribution of grant funding to SMEs significantly impacts their sustainability in the post-apartheid South African context. Some scholarly perspectives may neglect factors beyond grant provision that contribute to business success; however, evidence suggests that strategically deployed government support can stimulate economic prosperity. The effectiveness of grant schemes for small businesses in addressing systemic challenges within South African society is a complex interaction of political and policy factors. This chapter deconstructs different aspects of governmental financial support schemes, using stakeholder theory to highlight the various perspectives involved. The analysis examines whether the declared objectives of these grants emphasise political aims or authentically aim to promote sustainable development. The chapter analyses the literature and empirical evidence from studies examining the effects of government support since 1994. Many studies present counterintuitive data, underscoring the necessity for a nuanced understanding of the factors contributing to business success. The chapter emphasises the need to enhance the business ecosystem via evidence-based policy, ensuring that interventions are informed by a comprehensive understanding of the challenges encountered by small enterprises.

Chapter Three conducts a critical analysis of the progress made in supporting Black-owned businesses and evaluates the effectiveness of this funding in reducing disparities within historically marginalised communities. This research employed secondary data sourced from the Department of Trade and Industry (DTI), which included information on all granted awards, their designated purposes, and evaluations of their efficacy. This chapter analyses the effectiveness of equity and affirmative action laws in fund allocation to small business owners, focusing on the socio-demographic characteristics of grant recipients. The analysis is informed by social justice theory, providing a framework for examining the application of equity and equality in small businesses in South Africa. The findings reveal a troubling trend: a misunderstanding and misalignment in the practical application of equity and equality principles during the financial implementation phase, particularly evident during the COVID-19 pandemic. This highlights a discrepancy between policy goals and real-world conditions, stressing the need for a more refined and context-sensitive grant allocation process.

Chapter Four objectively examines the success of sponsored small businesses and compares their routes before and after 1994. The chapter examines the effectiveness of grant schemes in post-colonial South Africa and delves into great length on the politicisation and corruption that are often associated with sponsoring small enterprises. Contrary to some literature advocating for creating new funding formulas and assessment tools to improve the efficacy of state grant support programmes, this chapter takes a different approach. It examines how much South Africa's historical backdrop has influenced the development and implementation of grant programmes over the last thirty years. Although pre-colonial literature gives essential insights into the historical context of business funding, this chapter focuses on business performance statistics following government sponsorship. Taking a historical perspective, the chapter highlights the need to understand the socio-political context in which business policies are developed and executed. The major outcome underlines the need to shift grant rules away from privileged knowledge and towards merit-based standards. This adjustment is expected to have an impact on the efficiency and fair distribution of grant support programmes in South Africa.

Chapter Five examines the justification for subsidies directed towards predominantly Black suppliers and companies, acknowledging their significance in mitigating ongoing issues related to capital accumulation. The sustainability of these initiatives relies on accountability, underscoring its essential function in distributing and allocating funding and support. On the one hand, accountability starts with the government and encompasses a fair distribution of funds and subsidies. On the other hand, grant beneficiaries are also expected to demonstrate a complete understanding of grant criteria and their responsible application. This chapter develops a framework of grant provisioning based on allocation, distribution, and distribution concepts to identify challenges around funding and accountability in South Africa.

Chapter six explores the literature on government grant programmes, showing the need for partnerships to build trust within South Africa's business funding environment. Studies often highlight issues surrounding the misappropriation and mismanagement of public funds, as well as the duplicity involved in resource allocation. This chapter provides a detailed examination of the studies, classifying them according to arguments of economic determinism. Moreover, it argues that ongoing engagement with complex issues and a commitment to accountability for those in power are essential for enhancing funding systems in developing nations such as South Africa. The chapter, therefore, advocates for the establishment of strategic collaborations among diverse stakeholders. Higher education institutions, research institutes, and non-governmental organisations ought to establish partnerships to foster a collaborative strategy for reforming South Africa's existing funding concepts and practices.

9 Concluding Remarks

Considering South Africa's post-apartheid SME experience, a detailed study of funding solutions is essential. Its success will be determined by meticulous scrutiny of the programme objectives, qualification terms, and actual utilisation of accepted funds. It is imperative to establish whether these funds offer some development outcomes. Further, it is essential to analyse thoroughly the beneficiaries' populations and the large number of recipients. Forming an inclusive framework of accountability and offering clear spending of finances documented in Rand is also vital. All these, in concert, impact the achievement of efforts directed towards enabling corporate growth post-apartheid.

Such research involves the need for three-decade longitudinal data with information on the effect of intervention policies and the factors impacting them. While academic literature, more often than not, identifies shortcomings in government programmes, there is certainly a deficiency of large dataset analysis available to support such claims.

A sensitive issue is the political environment of business expansion, especially different political parties' views on economic change. Contradictory standpoints among political parties negatively impact policymaking. As a result, ideological tensions are caused by the split between left-of-centre and hard-right political camps.

The long-term economic consequences of a protectionist approach favouring domestic companies at the expense of foreign competitors are clear. Typically considered to be in the interest of long-term economic transformation, it is a fairer strategy that deliberately protects small businesses while enhancing market competition. However, this balance needs parliamentary consensus regarding the impact of immigration, foreign direct investment, and local businesses.

Disagreement in South Africa has caused social unrest and occasionally violence. Government interventions would thus have to be strategic to catalyse economic growth domestically and enhance global cooperation. Beyond simple economic marginalisation, the legacy of apartheid is broadly recognised to have created a state of 'incapacitation' that now constrains the individual and professional development of disadvantaged communities.

Policy is thus shaped to empower persons who have been disadvantaged under the conditions of economic oppression. Although they have provided vital emergency support, social handouts have contributed to reinforcing the dependency culture, precluding self-reliance and community-initiated projects from emerging. The spread of such subsidies can risk perpetuating the cycle of poverty at the cost of matching investments in economic and individual growth. Economic policies post-apartheid need to extend beyond simplistic cash handouts. Rather, they should prioritise establishing long-term economic prospects that empower individuals and help rebuild communities as a whole.

Funding from the government must effectively be revamped to encourage job creation and entrepreneurial activity. An analysis of long-term measures of government projects will assist in determining the extent to which this actually occurs. Data collected during this study will provide the groundwork for an in-depth policy analysis of small business loans in South Africa.

References

Abaquita, M. E., Hinayon, D. E., & Adriatico, C. G. (2024). Prospects and challenges in the implementation of barangay micro business enterprise program in the Philippine countryside. *Journal of Management, Economics, and Industrial Organization, 8*(1), 110–139.

Balkaran, S. (2017). Radical economic transformation-government prioritising state resources for small business development (SBD). *Journal of Management & Administration, 2017*(1), 105–128.

Baloyi, F., & Khanyile, M. B. (2022). Innovative mechanisms to improve access to funding for the black-owned small and medium enterprises in South Africa. *Southern African Journal of Entrepreneurship and Small Business Management, 14*(1), 1–14.

Bell, J., Goga, S., Mondliwa, P., & Roberts, S. (2018). *Structural Transformation in South Africa: Moving Towards a Smart, Open Economy for All* (CCRED Working Paper No. 9/2018). Social Science Research Network. https://ssrn.com/abstract=3269732 or https://doi.org/10.2139/ssrn.3269732

Bhorat, H., Buthelezi, M., Chipkin, I., Duma, S., Mondi, L., Peter, C., & Friedenstein, H. (2017). *Betrayal of the promise: how South Africa is being stolen*. State Capacity Research Project.

Bushe, B. (2019). The causes and impact of business failure among small to micro and medium enterprises in South Africa. *Africa's Public Service Delivery and Performance Review, 7*(1), 1–26.

Cant, M. C., & Wiid, J. A. (2013). Establishing the challenges affecting South African SMEs. *The International Business & Economics Research Journal (Online), 12*(6), 707.

Charalambous, M., Fryer, P. J., Panayides, S., & Smith, M. (2015). Implementation of food safety management systems in small food businesses in Cyprus. *Food Control, 57*, 70–75.

Christopher, M., & Towill, D. R. (2002). Developing market specific supply chain strategies. *The international journal of logistics management, 13*(1), 1–14.

Clack, W., & Minnaar, A. (2018). Rural crime in South Africa: an exploratory review of 'farm attacks' and stock theft as the primary crimes in rural areas. *Acta Criminologica: African Journal of Criminology & Victimology, 31*(1), 103–135.

Department of Small Business Development. (2020). *Annual report 2019/20. Republic of South Africa*. Retrieved April 13, 2024, from https://www.gov.za/documents/annual-reports/department-small-business-development-annual-report-20192020-04-nov-2020%20Government%20of%20South%20Africa+1

Du Toit, A., & Neves, D. (2017). The government of poverty and the arts of survival: mobile and recombinant strategies at the margins of the south African economy. In *New directions in agrarian political economy* (pp. 193–214). Routledge.

Ekene, A. K., & Kelly, T. D. (2023). Opportunities, challenges and risks: The South African business environment profiling opportunities and challenges of running small and medium-sized businesses in the post-apartheid Vhembe District of the Limpopo Province of South Africa. *Sustainable and Responsible Business in Africa: Studies in Ethical Leadership*, 41–61.

Enterprise Singapore. (2020). *Annual report 2019/2020*. Retrieved March 11, 2024, from https://www.enterprisesg.gov.sg/-/media/esg/files/resources/publications/annual-reports/esg_ar2019_20.pdf?la=en

Fatoki, O. O. (2012). The impact of ethics on the availability of trade credit to new small and medium sized enterprises (SMEs) in South Africa. *Journal of Social Sciences, 30*(1), 21–29.

Fielden, S. L., Davidson, M. J., & Makin, P. J. (2000). Barriers encountered during micro and small business start-up in north-West England. *Journal of Small Business and Enterprise Development, 7*(4), 295–304.

Gamede, B. T., & Uleanya, C. (2017). The role of entrepreneurship education in secondary schools at further education and training phase. *Academy of Entrepreneurship Journal, 23*(2).

Gardner, H. (2006). *Changing minds: The art and science of changing our own and other peoples minds*. Harvard Business Review Press.

Goga, S., Mondliwa, P., & Roberts, S. (2019). *Online retailing in South Africa: An overview*. (CCRED Working Paper No. 2/2019), University of Johannesburg.

Hetherington, K. (1994). The contemporary significance of Schmalenbach's concept of the bund. *The sociological review, 42*(1), 1–25.

Hocoy, D. (2020). Clinical implications of racial identity in the legacy of apartheid in South Africa. In *Merging past, present, and future in cross-cultural psychology* (pp. 308–322). Garland Science.

Irene, B. N. O. (2017). The macroeconomic landscape of post-apartheid South Africa a critical review of the effect of the broad-based black economic empowerment (BBBEE) program on the success of female SMEs operators. *Journal of Educational and Social Research, 7*(1), 145–150.

Joseph, T., Obikaonu, P., Ariolu, C., Nwolisa, C., & Aderohunmu, A. (2021). Smes intervention programmes in Nigeria: evaluating challenges facing implementation. *Applied Journal of Economics, Management and Social Sciences, 2*(1), 16–25.

Kongolo, M. (2010). Job creation versus job shedding and the role of SMEs in economic development. *African Journal of Business Management, 4*(11), 2288.

Ladzani, W. (2010). Historical perspective of small business development initiatives in South Africa with special reference to Limpopo province. *Problems and perspectives in management*, (8, Iss. 3), 68–79.

Lee, N. (2014). What holds back high-growth firms? Evidence from UK SMEs. *Small Business Economics, 43*(1), 183–195.

Lekaba, F. (2023). The impact of intra-party conflicts on the electoral performance of the all basotho convention in lesotho's 2022 elections. *JournaL of african ELEctions, 82.*

Mbonyane, B., & Ladzani, W. (2011). Factors that hinder the growth of small businesses in South African townships. *European business review, 23*(6), 550–560.

National Treasury. (2020). *Budget review 2020. Republic of South Africa.* Retrieved June 4, 2024, from https://www.treasury.gov.za/documents/national%20budget/2020/review/fullbr.pdf

Nel, E., & Rogerson, C. M. (2016). The contested trajectory of applied local economic development in South Africa. *Local Economy, 31*(1–2), 109–123.

Nengomasha, C. (2021). Post-apartheid cities in South Africa: A mirage of inclusivity. In *Urban Inclusivity in Southern Africa* (pp. 163–191).

Njue, N. G. (2021). *Implementation of Jua-kalis-empowerment Programme, Risk Management Practice and Performance of Micro-small-entrepreneurial Projects in Nairobi County, Kenya* (Doctoral dissertation). University of Nairobi.

Odeku, K. O., & Rudolf, S. S. (2019). An analysis of the transformative interventions promoting youth entrepreneurship in South Africa. *Academy of Entrepreneurship Journal, 25*(4), 1–10.

OECD. (2019). *OECD SME and entrepreneurship outlook 2019.* Retrieved February 23, 2024, from https://www.oecd.org/en/publications/oecd-sme-and-entrepreneurship-outlook-2019_34907e9c-en.html

Otache, I., & Usman, T. O. (2024). Entrepreneurial management, competitive advantage and SME performance: Evidence from an emerging economy. *European Business Review, 36*(6), 997–1014.

Rens, V., Iwu, C. G., Tengeh, R. K., & Esambe, E. E. (2021). SMEs, economic growth, and business incubation conundrum in South Africa. A literature appraisal. *Journal of Management and Research, 8*(2), 214–251.

Rogerson, C. M. (2008). Tracking SMME development in South Africa: Issues of finance, training and the regulatory environment. In *Urban forum* (Vol. 19, No. 1, pp. 61–81). Springer Netherlands.

Roper, S. (1997). Product innovation and small business growth: a comparison of the strategies of German, UK and Irish companies. *Small Business Economics, 9*, 523–537.

Schneider, F., & Medina, L. (2018). *Shadow economies around the world: What did we learn over the last 20 years?* (IMF Working Paper No. 18/17).

International Monetary Fund. https://www.imf.org/en/Publications/WP/Issues/2018/01/25/Shadow-Economies-Around-the-World-What-Did-We%20Learn-Over-the-Last-20-Years-45583%20IMF

Sebake, B. K. (2017). Neoliberalism in the South African post-apartheid regime: Economic policy positions and globalisation impact. In *International Conference on Public Administration and Development Alternatives (IPADA)*.

SEDA (Small Enterprise Development Agency). (2016). *The small, medium and micro enterprise sector of South Africa*. (Research Note 2016/01). Bureau for Economic Research, University of Stellenbosch. Retrieved June 20, 2024, from https://www.seda.org.za/Publications

Seekings, J. (2008). Deserving individuals and groups: the post-apartheid state's justification of the shape of South Africa's system of social assistance. *Transformation: Critical Perspectives on Southern Africa, 68*(1), 28–52.

Seekings, J., & Nattrass, N. (2011). State-business relations and pro-poor growth in South Africa. *Journal of International Development, 23*(3), 338–357.

Shackleton, C. M., Blair, A., De Lacy, P., Kaoma, H., Mugwagwa, N., Dalu, M. T., & Walton, W. (2018). How important is green infrastructure in small and medium-sized towns? Lessons from South Africa. *Landscape and Urban Planning, 180*, 273–281.

Sishuba, L. C. (2020). Institutional framework for promoting and supporting small, micro and medium enterprise in South Africa: supply perspective.

Smith, J. L. (2022). Continuing processes of uneven development in post-apartheid South Africa. *African Geographical Review, 41*(2), 168–188.

Ssekitoleko, P., & du Plessis, Y. (2021). Unravelling the makings for entrepreneurial success: A case study of the Maponya business in South Africa. *The Southern African Journal of Entrepreneurship and Small Business Management, 13*(1), 424.

Thaba-Nkadimene, K. L., Molotja, W., & Mafumo, T. N. (2019). The scourge of poverty among south African rural women: in defence of social justice. *Journal of Gender, Information and Development in Africa (JGIDA), 8*(3), 69–89.

UNDP (2022). *Africa sustainable development report 2022: Building back better from the coronavirus disease (covid-19) while advancing the full implementation of the 2030 agenda for sustainable development*. https://www.Undp.org. Retrieved March 23, 2024, from https://digitallibrary.un.org/record/4046861?v=pdf

Vivek, N. D. (2024). Transformation deferred: Disparate development in post-apartheid South Africa (1994-2004). *PanAfrican Journal of Governance and Development (PJGD), 5*(1), 128–155.

Walker, C. C., Druckman, A., & Jackson, T. (2021). Welfare systems without economic growth: A review of the challenges and next steps for the field. *Ecological Economics, 186*, 107066.

CHAPTER 2

Predictors of Grant Success for Small and Medium Enterprises in South Africa

1 Introduction

A realistic framework for predicting future economic trends may be found in the longitudinal examination of grant allocation and support systems for small and medium enterprises (SMEs). According to Abisuga-Oyekunle et al. (2020), small and medium-sized enterprises (SMEs) are becoming more recognised as vital contributors to sustainable development. It is anticipated that the operational activities of SMEs will substantially impact the elimination of poverty. On the other hand, modelling key economic performance indicators (KPIs) for the success of a business has proven to be a substantial issue. Incorporating interconnected variables is necessary to construct models that accurately simulate the economic implications of funding for small and medium-sized enterprises (SMEs). When the parameters of these models are stated appropriately, they have the potential to offer predictive insights about the long-term economic sustainability of a variety of environments, including South Africa. The incorporation of various and frequently complicated performance indicators is a common practice. This practice might introduce difficulties

The original version of the chapter has been revised. A correction to this chapter can be found at
https://doi.org/10.1007/978-981-95-2864-6_7

T. O. Aluko, *Evaluation of Small Business Support in Post-Apartheid South Africa*, https://doi.org/10.1007/978-981-95-2864-6_2

that require in-depth empirical inquiry in order to provide clarification. According to Prasannath et al. (2024), small and medium-sized enterprises (SMEs) are substantially tied to implementing appropriate support systems to encourage long-term sustainability. One of the most important questions is the connection between the various types of support, the performance of small and medium-sized enterprises (SMEs), and larger macroeconomic goals such as the elimination of poverty and the expansion of the economy. Due to the fact that the South African government has been investing in small and medium-sized enterprises (SMEs) for more than thirty years, it is necessary to conduct a comprehensive analysis of the success of these long-term interventions (Bushe, 2019). In order to boost economic growth, the government's support measures for small and medium-sized enterprises (SMEs) pay particular attention to the sector's variety. While this is going on, the economy's growth is contingent on whether or not the support that is obtained effectively accelerates the operations of SMEs towards improved performance. According to this point of view, performance comprises the transformational development of these companies, which the expansion of their operational size may demonstrate, the augmentation of their revenue, and a more substantial positive influence on the larger socio-economic environment. According to the literature (Iwu & Opute, 2019), the government's aims emphasise that the growth of small and medium-sized enterprises (SMEs) can influence the reduction of unemployment and poverty on a national scale. This is because the expansion of SMEs can increase revenue streams. To accurately estimate the influence of grants or other forms of support on the activities and economic performance of small and medium-sized enterprises (SMEs), it is essential to implement strategies that model and analyse the interconnected variables. Therefore, grasping the contextual particularities of small and medium-sized enterprises (SMEs) in South Africa is vital for a comprehensive grasp of such concerns.

2 Overview of Small and Medium Enterprises (SMEs) in South Africa

According to Kganyago (2022), the National Small Business Act of 1996 defines a small business in South Africa that considers the company's turnover, the size of its operations, and the industry sector. There has been a growing trend towards acknowledging small and medium-sized businesses (SMEs) as significant development drivers in several nations.

According to Abe et al. (2015), the expansion of small companies in the Czech Republic has been a significant factor in bolstering rural economies and fostering the growth of the local economy. According to Sarvari et al. (2021), the development of small businesses is an essential component for the success of construction companies in an Iranian context. The economic progress witnessed in Germany, which is widely acknowledged as a notable economy in Europe, can be partially linked to the developmental significance of the country's small and medium-sized enterprise (SME) sector (Herr & Nettekoven, 2018). Both industrialised and developing nations have used the strategic implementation of well-formulated policies for small and medium-sized enterprises (SMEs) to attain greater economic success and reduce the number of people living in poverty. According to Rens et al. (2021), South Africa acknowledged small and medium-sized enterprises (SMEs) as a crucial focal point for programmes facilitating transformative economic development after 1994. Policies in this country are supposed to foresee the role that small and medium-sized enterprises (SMEs) will play in achieving crucial macroeconomic goals, particularly in economic development and innovation. The contribution of small and medium-sized enterprises (SMEs) to South Africa's Gross Domestic Product (GDP) and overall employment figures is statistically significant (Pulka & Gawuna, 2022). During the previous few decades, it is estimated that this contribution has accounted for around 34 per cent of South Africa's gross domestic product. Since 1994, small and medium-sized businesses (also known as SMEs) have been responsible for around sixty per cent of the overall growth in employment in the country. In the post-apartheid setting of South Africa, the effect of small and medium-sized enterprises (SMEs) plays a crucial role in the creation of grassroots employment, which has contributed to a reduction in poverty; however, this drop will require further investigation for further analysis. According to the most recent unemployment and poverty rates data, this situation may be considered contradictory. Indeed, this position shows that stagnation or the negative repercussions of socio-economic transformational measures are occurring. Considering the growth of South Africa's economy from the point of view of small and medium-sized enterprises (SMEs), it is of the utmost importance to assess the amount to which these sectors contribute to or affect employment and poverty in the country.

The existing body of research indicates that small and medium-sized enterprises (SMEs) in South Africa are confronted with ongoing issues, the most significant of which is their inability to gain access to financial support or resources, primarily as a result of the legislative frameworks that are now in place (Msomi & Olarewaju, 2021). Financial institutions give applicants the highest priority regarding their capacity to efficiently use the funds and repay their loans with both principal and interest. Especially in the event of significant loan amounts, these severe standards necessitate the execution of complex application processes, which include comprehensive checklists that need the provision of collateral. Obtaining clearance for a loan is essential for capitalisation; nevertheless, navigating economic turmoil in the face of rising interest rates and inflation is another significant obstacle that must be overcome. One of the most common arguments in the discussion is that the government should intervene in the financial markets to alleviate the pressures that financial institutions are experiencing. This is especially true for small businesses without established credit records or strong asset bases for loan security. Similar difficulties have been reported in other countries, including Namibia (Baporikar et al. 2016), Ghana (Thompson Agyapong et al. 2018), Bangladesh (Chowdhury & Alam, 2017), and throughout the Asian and Pacific region (Abe, Troilo, and Batsaikhan, 2015). South Africa is not the only country facing difficulties in acquiring sufficient funding. One thing that all of these nations have in common is that they are considered to be emerging economies (Megersa, 2020). This suggests that the scale of their economic infrastructure substantially impacts their capacity to finance the development of small and medium-sized enterprises (SMEs) effectively. The government nonetheless holds a vital role in ensuring that financial connections between banks and small enterprises are established without undue exploitation of either party. This is so even though the government acknowledges the genuine worries that financial institutions have over the possibility of losses resulting from difficulties in debt collection.

These challenges are further compounded by global financial distress and political problems that have substantially strained South Africa's economy over the past decades. Developed countries have encouraged foreign investments to inject money into the economy. This policy imperative has necessitated the creation of enabling environments characterised by factors such as facilitated market access and discernible opportunities for growth for foreign investors. The South African government, however, needs to strategically ensure that foreign direct investment can serve as a mechanism for redirecting economic opportunities and/or utilising revenue generated from these relationships to augment budgetary allocations for small business development. Nevertheless, concern persists that the operational viability of SMEs might be compromised not due to inherent managerial inadequacies but rather as a consequence of broader economic challenges that have led to a contraction in the purchasing power and disposable incomes of the populace. Consequently, the government must identify and implement strategies that empower SMEs to effectively contribute to employment generation, poverty reduction, and the amelioration of other prevailing economic issues. In turn, the government should be positioned to provide or enhance the provision of grants to SMEs facilitated through banking institutions or other appropriate channels. This funding is expected to help entrepreneurs start new ventures or develop an existing business project into a large business. On the other hand, business growth and expansion require the structural efficacy of their management and leadership in translating strategic visions into productive realities. From this perspective, productivity refers to the manner in which companies use both financial and human resources to gain a significant market share within their segments, which requires a comprehensive understanding of marketing principles, pricing, and product development strategies, among other essential business functions.

Historically, the South African government has supported SMEs from the agriculture and transport sectors to strengthen the local economy (Fiseha & Oyelana, 2015). This support aimed to promote innovation in the South African economy and long-term global competitiveness. However, the funding strategies employed have been criticised for lacking a comprehensive and integrated framework, which may impede the government's ability to achieve corresponding outcomes (Du Plessis & Marnewick, 2017). The existing literature has not conclusively demonstrated that recipients of these grants consistently have the necessary business skills and prior experience to successfully meet the goals of their enterprises and the governmental entities supplying the funding (Rambe & Mosweunyane, 2017).

An important aspect is that the government generally does not anticipate repayment of the funding allocated to SMEs, which contrasts significantly with conventional bank financing or loan agreements. Although seemingly altruistic, the absence of a repayment obligation may unintentionally reduce the accountability and responsibility associated with government-funded SME initiatives. As a result, SMEs may lack the same urgency to maximise efforts for business sustainability since failure does not involve the forfeiture of personal capital or the requirement to repay the funds received. Conversely, funding models in various emerging and developing nations frequently link financial assistance to attaining specific milestones or established targets, potentially positioning SMEs more favourably to obtain subsequent funding rounds (Ndiaye et al. 2018). While government funding provides small business owners with non-high-risk financing opportunities, it also introduces challenges concerning accountability and the prudent allocation of funds for revenue generation and business expansion. Thus, government funding provides cash flows; however, its discontinuation, primarily if not strategically utilised to create sustainable revenue, frequently forces SMEs to pursue loans from banks. These institutions generally mandate prior financial statements and proof of effective fund management.

Systemic deprivation of opportunities, including equitable access to funding for entrepreneurial ventures, has been a historical reality for the Black population in South Africa (Makwara, 2019). As a result, a substantial portion of governmental initiatives has been focused on fostering economic activity in rural provinces and supporting Black-owned small enterprises (Musabayana & Mutambara, 2022). This policy orientation indicates the necessity of promoting a more equitable socio-economic environment. The purpose of governmental funding and programmes is to enable business owners to develop innovative business concepts that contribute to the economic development of their local area. Likewise, these initiatives are designed to facilitate the access of businesses and to assist and promote the development of new business concepts, thereby enabling the participation of disadvantaged communities in the mainstream economy of South Africa. Additionally, grants can function as a motivating factor, potentially resulting in positive outcomes by enabling the reallocation of resources from low-productive sectors to those with more significant potential for economic development (Kransdorff, 2010). Business grants must be tailored to the specificities of the rural context for disadvantaged communities to achieve sustainable development and grow out of poverty. Nevertheless, there is insufficient evidence to suggest that existing grant formulas and strategies adequately account for the diverse operational contexts of SMEs. Therefore, they may be operating under the assumption of homogeneity regarding demographics and the ability to utilise funding effectively. In essence, funding may be allocated without providing complementary support strategies to improve its suitability and effectiveness for small business proprietors in disadvantaged communities. SMEs in rural communities must understand how to access funding, its appropriate application, and vital information about business registration and the tax implications of their operations. In contrast, urban businesses and entrepreneurs are often better equipped to confront these obstacles with minimal or no external assistance due to their higher levels of education and proximity to governmental agencies and resources. These issues point to the need to re-examine how the funding framework for small businesses can be equitable and fair.

The main objective of governmental grant allocation appears to lack a focus on empowering business owners to use funds effectively. Developing this capacity is essential for entrepreneurial ventures' success and ongoing growth. This indicates that the current policy framework for SME finance has predominantly neglected to incorporate outcome-based measures in the financial support of small enterprises across the country. Governments seem to assume directionality and think linearly regarding social programmes or interventions. The supply of financial support to business owners is often presumed to be a sufficient requirement for achieving desired outcomes. This approach is political symbolism in policy literature, where government efforts focus entirely on policy text production rather than formulating effective implementation strategies. In the case of South Africa, the decision to allocate grants to business owners is based on the premise that providing financial resources to entrepreneurs will automatically result in favourable changes in the economic environment. Such ideologies neglect to recognise the lasting influence of South Africa's historical background in which many South Africans still have limited access to basic education and social amenities. Despite significant advancements over the past thirty years since democracy, the extent of this transformation may not justify the belief that businesses, especially in rural regions, can achieve desired outcomes solely through grants, absent additional training and targeted support. It is doubtful how policy frameworks can expect rural enterprises and their owners to conduct market research and complete feasibility assessments without specialised technical assistance. This discovery offers a plausible rationale for the ongoing recommendations indicating that a considerable percentage of business failures since the onset of democracy can be ascribed to an insufficient comprehension of pertinent policies and existing contextual realities.

3 Econometric Model

The use of econometric models helps the formulation of mathematical equations and prediction analyses for factors relevant to the study of financing small enterprises in the South African economic environment.

Specifically, linear regression statistics were used to test a hypothesis that the socio-demographic characteristics of business owners had a substantial influence on the utilisation patterns of financial subsidies granted to SMEs. This influence, in turn, is expected to shape how these funds are used to achieve more considerable economic advantages. Therefore, this model presents that the influence of the SME business owners (SBO) (SMB) and fund allocation strategy factor (1 FunStr) on Fund Usage (2FUSe) and the resultant economic benefits (3EcoB) can be represented mathematically.

Thus, the equation to help understand the model and its analysis is as follows:

$$\text{ECoB}it = \beta 0 + \beta 1\text{FunStr } it + \beta 2\text{FUSe}it + \varepsilon$$

$$\text{Economic benefits} = \beta 0 + \beta 1{}^{*}\text{education\_bg} + \beta 2{}^{*}\text{income\_hs} + \beta 3 \; {}^{*}\text{race} + \varepsilon$$

Using the analytical framework of stakeholder theory, this study attempted to define the relational structure established by the government as the funding institution, the allocated financial resources, and the recipients of these funds, with a particular emphasis on rural areas. This theoretical framework was utilised to analyse the extent to which these dynamics have influenced the outcomes of governmental grant allocation since 1994. Therefore, the corresponding representative equation is as follows:

$$\text{FundEcob} - \text{FundUse} = \text{EconB} = \beta 0 + \beta 1{}^{*}\text{Ecob} + \beta 2{}^{*}\ \text{SMEs\_rural} + \varepsilon - (\text{FundUseRural} = \beta 0 + \beta 1{}^{*}\ \text{Rural\_edu} + \beta 2{}^{*}\text{SMEs\_Inc\_Rural} + \varepsilon).$$

Regarding SMEs in rural communities and whether their location affects how funds are used to obtain economic benefits. The model considers different socio-demographic characteristics such as education and income. To predict how the demographic characteristics of Business Owners impact the usage of funds, variables such as SME owners' educational background, house income, and racial group will be modelled as follows:

$$\text{EcoB} = \beta 0 + \beta 1{}^{*}\text{SMEs Loction} + \beta 2{}^{*}\text{SMEs\_LocUbn} + \varepsilon\text{SME\_Rural} + \beta 0 + \beta 1{}^{*}\text{Income} + \beta 2{}^{*}\text{Education} + \varepsilon$$

a. Only data for the first five months of 2022/23 was available at the time of publication.

b. Indicator discontinued.

c. Indicator revised per the department's 2022/23 annual performance plan.

Based on the data in Table 1, the independent variable for this analysis consists of performance indicators obtained from various governmental programmes. The sample included various economic sectors and the range of development finance instruments utilised by government entities to support SMEs through 2023. The sampling framework included metrics such as the number of women-owned businesses receiving support, the quantity of SMMEs and cooperatives linked to global market opportunities, the provision of business infrastructure to SMMEs and cooperatives, the total value of support allocated to enterprises in township and rural areas, and the number of township and rural enterprises receiving both financial and non-financial support. This sampling strategy facilitates a thorough understanding of the government's financing model and the resulting changes observed across different economic sectors and within the demographic profile of SME owners due to the funding received.

Macroeconomic performance is the primary metric for the dependent variable. This allows for determining governmental support for SMEs on the trajectory of Gross Domestic Product (GDP) growth during the designated period. The longitudinal data (see Table 2) covers the percentage of change in essential macroeconomic indicators, such as consumption, expenditure, real GDP, and inflation, from 2019 to 2025.

Regarding exogenous variables, the analysis posits that the geographical allocation of governmental financial resources among provinces can serve as a proxy for evaluating policy effectiveness and each province's contributions to national development based on the support extended to SME owners from 2022 to 2026. Table 3 presents a comprehensive summary of the proportional distribution of financial resources the government allocates to eligible business proprietors. These data points reflect the government's and policymakers' intention to support SMEs across various contextual realities.

In light of the preceding discussion, Tables 1–3 are intended to elicit empirical data about the extent to which grants act as a predictor of both development and company success. Table 1 provides an overview of how the government supports SMEs in different economic sectors and their

Table 1 Mid-year performance as sampling.

Indicator	*Programme*	*MTSF priority*	*Annual performance*		
			Projected for 2022/23	*Achieved in the first half of 2022/23 (April to September)*	*Changed target for 2022/23*
Number of women-owned businesses supported to register on international platforms per year	Sector and market development	Priority 2: Economic transformation And job creation	2000	1044[a]	2500
Number of SMMEs and cooperatives linked to global market opportunities per year	Sector and market development		250	19	–
Number of SMMEs and cooperatives' business infrastructure refurbished or built per year	Sector and market development		6	1	–
Value of support provided to township and rural enterprises per year[b]	Development finance		R700m	–	–
Number of township and rural enterprises supported financially and/or non-financially per year[c]	Development finance		–	4341	20,000

(continued)

Table 1 (continued)

Indicator	*Programme*	*MTSF priority*	*Annual performance*		
			Projected for 2022/23	*Achieved in the first half of 2022/23 (April to September)*	*Changed target for 2022/23*
Number of crafters supported through the craft customised programme per year	Development finance		900	213	–
Value of support provided to cooperatives per year[b]	Development finance		R76.9 m	–	–
Number of cooperatives supported financially and/or non-financially per year[c]	Development finance		–	239	200

Source: Estimates of National Expenditure 2023—Vote 36: Small Business Development. https://www.treasury.gov.za/documents/mtbps/2022/aene/Vote%2036%20Small%20Business%20Development.pdf?utm_source

performance measures. Table 2 indicates the priorities of government financial distribution policies, whereas Table 3 illustrates the geographical allocation of support across provinces. The focal point in this chapter is the importance of grants for development and business success.

4 Grants as Predictors of Business Success

Examining the mechanisms by which financial support extended to SMEs across various provinces results in tangible developmental outcomes is a viable methodological approach to forecasting performance. Although the national-level measurement of performance and the projection of

Table 2 Macroeconomic performance and projection.

Calendar year *Percentage change*	*2019* *Actual*	*2020*	*2021*	*2022* *Estimate*	*2023* *Forecast*	*2024*	*2025*
Final household consumption	1,2	−5,9	5,6	2,9	1,6	1,7	1,8
Final government consumption	2,1	0,8	0,6	0,8	−1,8	−1,0	0,2
Gross fixed capital formation	−2,1	−14,6	0,2	4,0	1,9	3,6	3,8
Gross domestic expenditure	1,4	−8,0	4,8	3,6	1,2	1,6	1,8
Exports	−3,4	−11,9	10,0	7,4	1,9	2,8	2,9
Imports	0,4	−17,4	9,5	13,8	1,0	2,3	2,9
Real GDP growth	0,3	−6,3	4,9	1,9	1,4	1,7	1,8
GDP inflation	4,6	5,7	6,2	4,1	4,3	4,7	4,6
GDP at current prices (R billion)	5614	5557	6192	6572	6956	7406	7884
CPI inflation	4,1	3,3	4,5	6,7	5,1	4,6	4,6
Current account balance (% of GDP)	−2,6	2,0	3,7	0,2	−0,9	−1,1	−1,2

Source: National Treasury, Reserve Bank, and Statistics South Africa https://www.treasury.gov.za/documents/national%20budget/2023/review/BR%202023%20-%20Tables%20for%20chapter%202.xlsx?utm_source

Table 3 Provincial equitable share: Expenditure priority.

R million	*2022/23*	*2023/24*	*2024/25*	*2025/26*
Eastern cape	72,231	71,682	74,059	77,422
Free state	31,107	30,815	31,798	33,157
Gauteng	120,042	118,566	123,219	128,844
KwaZulu-Natal	114,558	113,240	116,758	121,688
Limpopo	64,056	64,175	66,774	70,276
Mpumalanga	45,962	45,834	47,581	49,882
Northern cape	14,942	14,878	15,441	16,182
North west	39,540	39,373	41,027	43,091
Western cape	58,367	57,822	59,844	62,359
Total	**560,805**	**556,385**	**576,501**	**602,900**

Source: National Treasury https://www.treasury.gov.za/documents/mtbps/2022/mtbps/FullMTBPS.pdf?utm_source

future trends are undoubtedly significant, the modelling of performance variables at the provincial level provides a valuable approach to comprehending the differentiated contributions of businesses within each province to the aggregate development of South Africa. Nevertheless, the term 'development' necessitates a comprehensive definition. In the South African context, development is frequently not defined broadly but more specifically concerning racial groups and, at times, integrating gender considerations. This specificity emphasises the critical role of race as a variable in the modelling of SME performance and its contribution to the economic development of South Africa. In addition, the policy frameworks that establish or commission funding or grant initiatives typically define the intended outcome of governmental financial support. A primary objective is frequently the strategic deployment of grants to achieve socio-economic transformation. This implies a policy assumption that providing financial resources to SMEs will result in a corresponding impact on reducing poverty and unemployment. These two significant socio-economic challenges have persisted in South Africa since 1994 with limited substantial alteration. Quality and corruption are frequently identified as significant factors contributing to these persistent problems in the existing literature. Nevertheless, the degree to which these factors have impacted SMEs, whether positively or negatively, is a subject that necessitates additional research. If SMEs have made a positive contribution, it is also necessary to quantify the level or percentage of this contribution to reducing destitution and unemployment.

Socio-economic inequality is a prevalent feature of the South African environment, affecting various aspects of society, including the allocation of social welfare payments and entrepreneurship subsidies among racial groups. The Black African population historically faced institutional exclusion and discriminatory laws that hindered their economic progress, a period known as apartheid. In recent decades, especially after 1994, transformation agendas and policies were enacted to redress past inequalities and guarantee equitable opportunities for all South African citizens, regardless of race and location. This table (see appendix) shows that after 1994 or from 2008 to 2017, a substantial disparity remains among Black Africans relative to other racial groups despite the introduction of multiple governmental interventions. This leads to an inquiry about how grants can effectively stimulate economic growth, notwithstanding persistent systemic inequities in South Africa.

In South Africa, the use of grants to support SMEs has been a widespread but contentious practice in democratic South Africa, with claims that these grants do not always yield favourable economic results in accordance with specific programme objectives. The degree to which the overall advantages of implementing such funding systems surpass their related expenses is still a matter of contention. Despite this disagreement, several governments globally persist in providing diverse grant financing schemes to tackle specific internal economic issues (Mazanai & Fatoki, 2011; Xiang & Worthington, 2013). Inadequate allocation of grant funding for programmes and inappropriate distribution of the funds affect programme efficiency. For example, funding programmes established for political reasons leads to programme distortion and inefficiency. Various government intervention programmes have been operating in South Africa for the last 30 years; however, due to the lack of evidence-based research, the study could not determine the entire cohort of problems and challenges associated with grant-funding programmes in the country.

The methodologies and protocols that guide the establishment and implementation of grant-funding programmes are crucial for assessing their overall success and effectiveness. To achieve optimal impact, grant-funding programmes require transparency, accessibility for eligible applicants, and clarity in their operational mechanisms and stipulations. This would justify the programmes' strategic purpose and individual participants' response toward the delivery and achievement of targeted goals. Below is a summary of various government intervention programmes in South Africa, including their aims, objectives, targeted beneficiaries, and criteria for enterprises.

4.1 Impacts of grants on GDP and FDI

The analysis of real per capita GDP growth in South Africa indicates a trend of decline or stagnation from 2012 to 2019, following an unsustainable peak in 2006 and a significant contraction in 2009, as shown in the accompanying table (see appendix). Per capita GDP indicates the share of national income attributable to everyone in South Africa, thereby illustrating the government's ability to distribute income to its citizens through diverse social and economic benefits. This decline indicates a decrease in the nation's economic output per capita, which may reflect underlying capacity constraints and contextualise the gradual reduction in social welfare provisions and the extent of governmental support for SMEs.

To achieve significant and lasting impact, SMEs must assess their operational success regarding profitability and measurable contributions to long-term sustainability. Profit is a critical factor, yet it should not be regarded as the only or ultimate measure of business success. However, its strategic reinvestment can promote additional revenue generation and business growth. In the modern context, profit and business growth are increasingly acknowledged as inadequate indicators of long-term sustainability for both the enterprise and society at large. A common argument asserts that businesses should actively generate value by making concrete contributions to environmental conservation and positive social outcomes resulting from their operations. A thorough evaluation of the effectiveness of business support in promoting sustainable futures for both direct beneficiaries and the broader society requires the examination of various interconnected factors.

Similar to other countries, the South African government can leverage Foreign Direct Investment (FDI) to attract vital financial resources to stimulate or bolster economic growth. An analysis of net foreign direct investment reveals a decrease from 2008 to 2017, as shown in the in the appendix, followed by a notable recovery from 2018 onwards; however, the magnitude of this increase has not sufficiently addressed the enduring systemic issues of poverty and inequality that have afflicted South Africa for decades. FDI usually involves the implementation of a policy framework that promotes establishing and encouraging foreign business entrance to South Africa to facilitate an influx of economic resources that may be judiciously used for national economic development. The decline in FDI shows either inadequate governmental attempts to attract foreign investment or the implementation of policy constraints that deter such inflows. Looking into the future, there may be a need to rethink policy in such a way as to ensure that FDI is promoted while protecting local businesses simultaneously.

The appendix shows that businesses' ability to find long-term funding for asset purchases declined between 2013 and 2015. Over that period, this negative tendency displayed no notable reversal. Businesses need regular and dependable capital generation for operational expansion to invest in necessary assets such as machinery, buildings, and equipment. Governmental interest rate policies, among other elements outside of a company's control, could make obtaining or creating this required capital difficult. The appendix table shows a constant interest rate environment—especially from 2012 to 2019—this consistency does not always translate to affordability for every borrower. Small business entrepreneurs starting new projects often find this to be true. The reality for small firms could be different even if the controlled interest rate environment would imply affordable borrowing rates. Their power to create enough income and profits from the acquired money determines their capacity to control borrowing expenses. Should interest rates continue to be a burden, it could indicate underlying problems with income creation and profitability, maybe driven by more general economic conditions and inflationary pressures.

Notwithstanding a period of relatively low inflation—mostly in 2018 based on current statistics (see table in the appendix)—the global economic scene has seen a general rise in the cost of goods and services following the COVID-19 epidemic, a trend also observed in South Africa. Businesses have had to rethink their pricing strategies to keep revenue generating, remain profitable, and control interest payments. Depending on the products sold and the company's location, higher prices can affect sales volumes and, hence, a company's capacity to fulfil its financial responsibilities. With the continuous development of technology drastically changing operating standards, the COVID-19 epidemic brought about extensive job losses and a significant upheaval of conventional company procedures. As consumer expectations about service delivery have changed, business owners who have not adequately adjusted to technology developments could thus find themselves at a disadvantage in profit generation. In essence, unemployment and inflation have degraded consumer buying power. Customers are still in a position to spend, which probably makes increasing the value and satisfaction of their purchases a top priority. As such, business owners must fully grasp the dynamics of these changing surroundings.

4.2 Risk Factors

Navigating the corporate terrain successfully means controlling both internal and external risk elements. Internal influences can include the socio-economic profile of business owners, including their education levels and upbringing, which might affect their approach to running small and medium-sized enterprises (SMEs). According to certain studies, especially in South Africa, demographic traits such as race and gender should not be the primary basis for assessing or projecting the success of SMEs. The premise is that those who have enough tools and education should be able to succeed regardless of their race or gender. This point of view, however, calls for more contextual knowledge and supporting empirical data. On the other hand, external factors can influence every business owner regardless of their attributes. Regardless of the owner's natural business sense, government laws on taxes and the general political framework can significantly affect the direction of SMEs. Still, appropriately trained individuals are usually more suited to meet and conquer these external variables than those without such readiness. Therefore, it is imperative to carefully analyse the internal and external risk variables at play while researching and modelling the possible impact of SMEs based on owner demographics.

Particularly for South African SMEs, a key component of reaching business success is owners' intentional efforts to increase their financial resources in order to generate employment possibilities. This means giving significant thought to the goods and services provided to guarantee both profitability and a good impact on the welfare of South Africans. Examining whether SME owners generally have the required training and practical experience can help determine whether they can make wise business decisions that would result in significant societal impact or financial success. Although entrepreneurs might look for funding for their projects, it is still a matter of debate whether pertinent policies sufficiently evaluate the applicant's skills and experience as possible indicators of their ability to use the resources and produce favourable results efficiently. Existing studies have indicated that a significant contributing cause to business failure may be insufficient training and related experience. Moreover, the kind and extent of knowledge and experience needed for SMEs to flourish also call for further consideration. Therefore, SME owners' educational background and training should be significant determinants in creating models and assessments of corporate success.

Evidence suggests a connection between the level of education entrepreneurs attain and the likelihood of their business success, as demonstrated by research conducted in the KwaZulu-Natal region. However, denying entrepreneurs financial grants solely based on their educational qualifications could be viewed as a means of reinforcing existing societal inequalities. This raises a moral question: Should SMEs presenting compelling business proposals, potentially indicated by the educational attainment of their owners, receive greater funding support? The underlying rationale is that empowering individuals with a more substantial knowledge base could enable them to more effectively contribute to the government's efforts in developing a vital sector where progress and impact are keenly needed and can be readily seen. Nevertheless, it is crucial to consider what knowledge or education level is required to run a company for profit and good influence. Although scholarly publications usually offer a general definition of education concerning corporate success, this definition should be further polished and contextualised to grasp better its particular significance and importance within the South African setting.

The age of small and medium-sized enterprise (SME) owners is a critical demographic characteristic intricately interwoven with their level of educational attainment, forming a complex tapestry that influences entrepreneurial endeavours and business outcomes. This interaction between age and education is not merely an academic curiosity but a practical consideration of substantial importance, particularly in the dynamic landscape of South Africa's evolving economy. The comprehension of the intricacies of this relationship is essential for policymakers, support organisations, and even aspiring entrepreneurs, as it illuminates the diverse needs, challenges, and potential of various cohorts within the SME sector.

An intriguing observation is made regarding the apparent reluctance of younger individuals to actively pursue governmental funding or other forms of assistance when they begin establishing their businesses. Although this reluctance may appear counterintuitive in light of such support's potential advantages, it is worth further investigation. A variety of factors may influence this phenomenon. Younger individuals may exhibit a higher level of self-reliance, which is motivated by a desire to demonstrate their capabilities independently. Alternatively, they may be underinformed about the specific governmental programmes and initiatives available or perceive the application processes as excessively bureaucratic, time-consuming, or intimidating. Despite the numerous benefits of the digital age, it may also lead to the belief that resources and solutions can be discovered within one's networks or through online platforms, potentially obscuring the more formal support structures the government provides. Additionally, this behaviour may be influenced by cultural factors or a general scepticism towards governmental intervention. The government must comprehend these fundamental motivations and perceptions to customise its outreach and support mechanisms to engage with this demographic effectively.

The South African government has acknowledged SMEs' critical role in promoting economic growth, generating employment opportunities, and promoting social development since the new democratic era in 1994. As a result, various support programmes and initiatives have been implemented over the years aimed at business owners in various sectors and categories. These interventions have consisted of financial assistance in the form of grants, loans, and tax incentives, as well as non-financial support in business development training, mentorship programmes, and access to markets. The government's dedication to cultivating the entrepreneurial spirit in young people and enabling them to become active participants in the economy is emphasised by the explicit incorporation of young individuals within these support frameworks.

Governmental initiatives have specifically targeted distinct sub-groups within the broad category of young entrepreneurs, acknowledging this demographic's diverse circumstances and requirements. One such category includes young individuals who, for a variety of reasons, were unable to conclude their high school education or who were unable to access formal education at all. Entrepreneurship is a potentially critical pathway to economic empowerment and self-sufficiency for these individuals, as they frequently encounter substantial obstacles to entry into the traditional labour market. The government may prioritise providing fundamental business skills training, vocational skills development, and access to micro-finance to assist this group in establishing and expanding small-scale enterprises. Recognising their potential despite their limited formal education is critical to inclusive economic development.

Young individuals who have intentionally chosen to become entrepreneurs are another significant category. This decision is frequently motivated by a passion for innovation, a desire for independence, or the recognition of unmet market requirements. Although these individuals may have varying degrees of formal education, they share a proactive decision to establish their course in the business world. Access to more advanced business development programmes, mentorship from experienced entrepreneurs, and platforms for networking and accessing funding opportunities are potential forms of government support for this group. Fostering a culture of innovation and promoting the development of high-growth potential businesses necessitates encouraging and supporting this segment of youthful entrepreneurs.

Additionally, there is a unique group of young individuals who, despite having successfully concluded their high school education or earning degrees from universities, have been unable to secure employment in the formal sector. This phenomenon of graduate unemployment is a substantial challenge in numerous economies, including South Africa, and can result in the underutilisation of valuable skills and knowledge and disillusionment. Entrepreneurship frequently presents itself as a viable and appealing alternative for these young graduates, enabling them to capitalise on their education and abilities to generate opportunities. Specialised business incubation programmes, access to seed funding, and guidance on traversing the complexities of starting and scaling a business are potential areas of government support specifically designed for this group. Their academic background frequently provides them with a robust theoretical foundation that, when combined with practical entrepreneurial skills, can result in the establishment of sustainable and innovative businesses.

Interestingly, despite the dissimilarities in their educational histories, the group of young individuals with limited formal education and young graduates transitioning to entrepreneurship are both regarded as 'youth'. This shared characteristic of adolescents frequently results in a greater probability of demonstrating a specific level of technology literacy and networking proficiency. In today's increasingly digital and interconnected world, the capacity to utilise technology for communication, marketing, operations, and information access is critical to the success of any business. Consequently, this presents a substantial advantage. Similarly, youthful entrepreneurs can establish relationships with customers, suppliers, mentors, and potential investors, which creates valuable support systems and opportunities for collaboration, thanks to their strong networking skills.

Nevertheless, the degree of technology literacy and networking proficiency can fluctuate considerably based on the environment in which these young individuals were raised and the specific circumstances of their upbringing. Their proficiency in these areas can be influenced by various factors, including supportive networks within their communities, exposure to digital tools and platforms, and access to technology infrastructure. Consequently, while it is generally accurate that newer generations have experienced a more technologically advanced era, it is crucial to avoid making broad generalisations and acknowledge the potential for disparities influenced by socio-economic backgrounds and geographical location.

In addition, it is generally undisputed that the younger generation today has access to many technological tools and information unavailable to previous generations during their formative years. An environment in which information is easily accessible and instantaneous communication has been established due to the proliferation of the internet, mobile devices, social media platforms, and a variety of software applications.

This digital fluency offers young entrepreneurs unparalleled opportunities to enhance their business operations, research markets, connect with consumers, and acquire new skills.

The government of South Africa is explicitly committed to leveraging the inherent potential of its youthful population to promote the growth of corporations and, in turn, to stimulate the country's overall economic development. The government's objective is to unleash the innovative capacity and dynamism of its young citizens, thereby transforming them into major drivers of economic progress, by cultivating an environment that supports youth entrepreneurship through targeted programmes, access to resources, and promoting a conducive regulatory framework.

Conversely, the precise influence of age on its own and in conjunction with varying degrees of formal education in determining business success is still a subject of ongoing scholarly inquiry. This is a multifaceted and intricate matter with many interacting variables. In the academic and policy communities, there is still much modelling, analysis, and discussion regarding how age moderates or interacts with factors such as education, experience, and access to resources, despite the logical assumption that these factors would significantly influence entrepreneurial outcomes. In order to develop a more sophisticated comprehension of these relationships, longitudinal studies that monitor the performance of businesses established by individuals of varying ages and educational backgrounds, in conjunction with rigorous statistical analysis, are required. Additionally, qualitative research that investigates the lived experiences and perspectives of entrepreneurs from differing age and educational cohorts can offer valuable insights into the factors that influence their success or failure.

5 Concluding Remarks

Studies show that a company's economic success cannot be guaranteed solely by financial support. Growing studies cast doubt on the theory that small and medium-sized businesses (SMEs) have a direct, simple link between finance and favourable results. Although funding is crucial, the reality is significantly more complicated, and many elements affect the path of a company. For SMEs, it is imperative to evaluate financial support in line with a broad spectrum of primarily external factors that can significantly impact the outcomes of government funding programmes. Often outside the direct control of the business owner, these factors might offer possibilities and obstacles influencing the efficacy of financial interventions.

We must transcend a simple input-output paradigm to grasp the effect of financial support. We have to acknowledge the dynamic interaction between finance and the bigger surroundings SMEs run inside. This covers macroeconomic situations, laws, market dynamics, and socio-political impacts. Regardless of their financial support, government policies, including labour laws, trade rules, and taxes, can significantly affect SMEs' operating expenses and profitability. Likewise, changes in consumer demand, competition pressures, and technology upheavals could offer chances and challenges influencing a company's capacity for growth.

Furthermore, socio-cultural elements that are very important for SMEs' success include access to education, social networks, and cultural perspectives on entrepreneurship. When education and training prospects are few, business owners could lack the skills and expertise to handle their money and negotiate market complexity properly. Likewise, SMEs could find it challenging to get resources and create the relationships required for expansion in settings where social networks are weak, or entrepreneurship is not particularly appreciated.

Therefore, while assessing the impact of financial support on SMEs, it is imperative to adopt a complete perspective that considers how these several outside factors interact. Rather than merely providing money, policymakers and financial agencies should establish an environment that promotes SMEs' long-term development and sustainability. This calls for a well-rounded plan encompassing SMEs' prospects and difficulties: market access, financing, skills and training, and a favourable legislative framework.

Although obtaining funding is a vital initial step in beginning a company, achieving long-term financial sustainability should be the main objective for companies running in South Africa; the absence of this might be a significant obstacle. Particularly in developing countries such as South Africa, access to finance is often blamed as a primary obstacle to entrance and expansion for SMEs. Entrepreneurs lacking funds could struggle to start their companies, make necessary equipment and technology investments, and grow their activities. Lack of funding can also hinder creativity and stop SMEs from realising their full potential to help generate employment and boost the economy.

It is as vital, though, to realise that financial access is not an end in and of itself. Simply subsidising SMEs without tackling the underlying problems that endanger their existence will not likely produce long-term success. Beyond just getting started, financial sustainability is a company's capacity to create sufficient money, control its costs, and keep profitability over the long run. Thus, strong bases in operational efficiency, strategic planning, and financial management are essential.

If SMEs want to reach financial sustainability, they must build strong business models capable of producing enough revenue to pay their expenses and produce a profit. This calls for a strong value offer, complete market awareness, and successful marketing and sales strategies. Smart cost management by SMEs also requires careful budgeting, cost control, and smart resource allocation. Developing good financial management techniques like precise record-keeping, cash flow management, and financial planning is especially vital for SMEs.

In this sense, 'sustainability' refers to making business decisions that maximise the use of given financial resources and create earnings that might be reinvested in the organisation's future growth. This definition underlines the requirement for careful use of resources and long-term financial planning. Sustainable SMEs are those which can effectively distribute their financial resources to guarantee their long-term survival and growth. Generating revenue is only one aspect of this; another is returning those profits to the business to boost its operations, enlarge its market share, and raise its competitiveness.

Moreover, the concept of sustainability reaches social and environmental obligations as well as financial ones. Sustainable SMEs run their businesses so that their negative environmental impact is minimised and their employee's and local communities' welfare is supported. This covers implementing environmentally sustainable policies, paying fair salaries and working conditions, and participating in socially conscious events.

For many SMEs, particularly in developing countries, reaching financial sustainability is challenging and tedious. Their range of constraints is sometimes limited access to resources, lack of managerial knowledge, and a difficult corporate environment. SMEs must create strong business strategies, use good management techniques, and establish close ties with their stakeholders if they go beyond these challenges.

Many small and medium-sized business owners battle in this area; they may get initial capital but lack the required support mechanisms to guarantee the long-term viability of their organisation, therefore restricting their potential to make a significant contribution. This draws attention to a major shortfall in the help accessible to SMEs. Fledgling companies depend on financial availability, but it is usually insufficient to ensure long-term survival. Hence, running a business and attaining consistent development call for a range of support systems for SMEs.

Business development services, training and mentoring programmes, market access, and technology support are just a few ways these support systems could manifest themselves. SMEs can get the knowledge and direction they need to draft strong company plans, enhance their marketing and sales tactics, and adequately handle their revenue from business development services. Programmes for mentorship and training will let managers and owners of SMEs acquire the tools required to run their companies successfully. Market access lets SMEs boost sales and widen their consumer base. Technological assistance can help SMEs adopt new technologies to enhance their efficiency and competitiveness.

Without these support mechanisms, SMEs are often left to fend for themselves, which can significantly increase their risk of failure. They may struggle to manage their finances effectively, access new markets, and adapt to changing market conditions. This hinders their growth and sustainability and limits their potential to contribute to economic development and job creation.

Therefore, governments, funding agencies, and other stakeholders must recognise the importance of providing comprehensive support to SMEs. This support should go beyond simply providing financial resources and instead focus on creating an enabling environment that fosters SMEs' long-term growth and sustainability. This requires a coordinated and integrated approach that addresses SMEs' challenges and opportunities, ensuring they have the resources and support needed to thrive.

In conclusion, while access to finance is a critical enabler for SMEs, it does not guarantee success. A holistic approach is needed to ensure SMEs' long-term viability and contribution, combining financial support with various other support mechanisms. This includes creating a supportive environment, providing business development services, facilitating market access, and promoting financial sustainability. By adopting such an approach, policymakers and stakeholders can help SMEs overcome their challenges and unlock their full potential to drive economic growth, create jobs, and contribute to sustainable development.

References

Abe, M., Troilo, M., & Batsaikhan, O. (2015). Financing small and medium enterprises in Asia and the Pacific. *Journal of Entrepreneurship and Public Policy, 4*(1), 2–32.

Abisuga-Oyekunle, O. A., Patra, S. K., & Muchie, M. (2020). SMEs in sustainable development: Their role in poverty reduction and employment generation in sub-Saharan Africa. *African Journal of Science, Technology, Innovation and Development, 12*(4), 405–419.

Baporikar, N., Nambira, G., & Gomxos, G. (2016). Exploring factors hindering SMEs' growth: Evidence from Namibia. *Journal of Science and Technology Policy Management, 7*(2), 190–211.

Bushe, B. (2019). The causes and impact of business failure among small to micro and medium enterprises in South Africa. *Africa's Public Service Delivery and Performance Review, 7*(1), 1–26.

Chowdhury, M., & Alam, Z. (2017). Factors affecting access to finance of Bangladesh's small and medium enterprises (SMEs). *USV Annals of Economics and Public Administration, 2*(26), 55.

Du Plessis, H., & Marnewick, A. (2017). A roadmap for innovative city services to address challenges small businesses face in South Africa. *South African Journal of Economic and Management Sciences, 20*(1), 1–18.

Fiseha, G. G., & Oyelana, A. A. (2015). An assessment of the roles of small and medium enterprises (SMEs) in the local economic development (LED) in South Africa. *Journal of Economics, 6*(3), 280–290.

Herr, H., & Nettekoven, Z. M. (2018). *The role of small and medium-sized enterprises in development: What can be learned from the German experience?* (Vol. No. 53). Global Labour University Working Paper.

Iwu, C. G., & Opute, A. P. (2019). Eradicating poverty and unemployment: Narratives of survivalist entrepreneurs. *Journal of Reviews on Global Economics, 8*, 1438–1451.

Kganyago, L. M. (2022). *"Personal service" and "professional service": The rigid application of turnover tax and small business corporation legislation.* (Master's thesis,. University of Pretoria.

Kransdorff, M. (2010). Tax incentives and foreign direct investment in South Africa. *Consilience*, (3), 68–84.

Makwara, T. (2019). Taking on the challenge: Small, micro and medium enterprises (SMMEs) and socio-economic development in South Africa. *African Journal of Hospitality, Tourism and Leisure, 8*(1), 1–14.

Mazanai, M., & Fatoki, O. (2011). The effectiveness of business development services (BDS) providers in improving access to debt finance by start-up SMEs in South Africa. *International Journal of Economics and Finance, 3*(4), 208–216.

Megersa, K. (2020). Improving SMEs' access to finance through capital markets and innovative financing instruments: Some evidence from developing countries. *Nairobi Securities Exchange website*. https://www.nse.co.ke

Msomi, T., & Olarewaju, O. (2021). Evaluation of access to finance, market and viability of small and medium-sized enterprises in South Africa. *Problems and Perspectives in Management, 19*(1), 281–289.

Musabayana, G. T., & Mutambara, E. (2022). The implementation of the broad-based black economic empowerment (B-BBEE) policy in South Africa: A myth or a reality in SMEs? *Australasian Accounting, Business and Finance Journal, 16*(1), 73–84.

Ndiaye, N., Razak, L. A., Nagayev, R., & Ng, A. (2018). Demystifying small and medium enterprises'(SMEs) performance in emerging and developing economies. *Borsa Istanbul Review, 18*(4), 269–281.

Prasannath, V., Adhikari, R. P., Gronum, S., & Miles, M. P. (2024). Impact of government support policies on entrepreneurial orientation and SME performance. *International Entrepreneurship and Management Journal, 20*, 1533–1595.

Pulka, B. M., & Gawuna, M. S. (2022). Contributions of SMEs to employment, gross domestic product, economic growth and development. *Jalingo Journal of Social and Management Sciences, 4*(1), 1–18.

Rambe, P., & Mosweunyane, L. (2017). A poverty-reduction oriented perspective to small business development in South Africa: A human capabilities approach. *African Journal of Science, Technology, Innovation and Development, 9*(3), 289–302.

Rens, V., Iwu, C. G., Tengeh, R. K., & Esambe, E. E. (2021). SMEs, economic growth, and business incubation conundrum in South Africa. A literature appraisal. *Journal of Management and Research, 8*(2), 214–251.

Sarvari, H., Chan, D. W., Alaeos, A. K. F., Olawumi, T. O., & Aldaud, A. A. A. (2021). Critical success factors for managing construction small and medium-sized enterprises in developing countries of Middle East: Evidence from Iranian construction enterprises. *Journal of Building Engineering, 43*, 103152.

Thompson Agyapong, G., Mmieh, F., & Mordi, C. (2018). Factors influencing the growth of SMEs: The case of Ghana. *Thunderbird International Business Review, 60*(4), 549–563.

Xiang, D., & Worthington, A. C. (2013). The impact of government financial assistance on SMEs in Australia during the GFC. *Journal of Griffith Business Schools, 7*, 2–5.

CHAPTER 3

Social Justice Analysis of Post-Apartheid Policies for Black-Owned Businesses

1 Introduction

The notion of social justice is frequently employed when discussing racial equality, the rights of individuals with disabilities, and the broader issue of societal inequality experienced by the Black population. Consequently, the meaning of social justice can be understood differently depending on the specific context (Juggernath, 2019). For small and medium enterprises (SMEs), the emphasis on equity and equality in resource allocation in South Africa demonstrates the government's objective of fostering a more equitable society through grants and various support initiatives. Still, in the post-apartheid era, a balanced approach incorporating equity financing to enhance diversity, and transformation is considered essential (Goga, Bosiu, & Bell, 2019). This entails carefully considering how policies are developed and the underlying notion of social justice that informs them. Following 1994, there was a significant hope that Black people would achieve economic parity and empowerment, which was considered a form of social justice to address the disadvantages imposed by White minority rule. In South Africa, Black empowerment is an important approach to promoting social justice (Makgoba, 2024). Therefore, the structure of grants for SMEs is often aligned with the goals of Black empowerment (Shava, 2016). The fundamental idea is to reclaim what was unjustly taken and return it to Black South Africans. The democratic government particularly emphasises land as an area requiring social

T. O. Aluko, *Evaluation of Small Business Support in Post-Apartheid South Africa*, https://doi.org/10.1007/978-981-95-2864-6_3

justice, given its forceful seizure (from Black people) during apartheid. As a result, the land reform agenda is an integral component of the broader transformation and Black empowerment efforts (Boudreaux, 2010). Land is recognised as a crucial asset for production, enabling activities like farming, construction, and business, all of which contribute to economic advancement. This signifies a move to redistribute wealth to Black communities. However, a significant portion of the Black population still feels they lack adequate control over land that could provide business opportunities and empower them economically. While this chapter does not delve into the specifics of land reform or ownership, land is a pertinent illustration of the ongoing struggle to achieve justice in areas with the potential for substantial economic empowerment for Black individuals. Access to suitable spaces for conducting business is vital. SMEs, especially those in the agricultural sector, might face persistent challenges in securing or expanding their operations without access to such land. Hence, addressing social justice in the context of SME funding requires a deep understanding of the fundamental issues surrounding the allocation of economic benefits in the period following 1994.

2 Funding Small Business as Social Justice

This intricate situation is inherently tied to political dynamics and policy decisions. Various political factions have expressed the necessity of tackling the underlying social justice issues rather than merely addressing its superficial aspects. The core of social justice lies within the realm of politics and the political commitment to address the concerns that the majority of the population identifies as significant in their daily lives. When the government-initiated programmes to support SMEs, South Africa harboured aspirations of achieving justice from historical economic oppression and attaining economic freedom by 2030 (Hassen, 2018). However, the essence of justice implies that it should be complete and not just a partial offering. By complete, it signifies that SMEs should experience genuine empowerment that extends beyond just receiving initial funding to start a business. They also seek the liberty to access a broader range of opportunities, such as securing business premises without facing exclusion, the ability to participate in business sectors that were historically dominated by White individuals without encountering discrimination, and various other factors that would foster a sense of true justice. Nevertheless, the government has a crucial regulatory function in facilitating economic freedom by providing financial support to small businesses (Graafland, 2019). In essence, every individual, irrespective of race, should have the unrestricted right to engage in business ventures that align with their capabilities, free from discrimination. When individuals feel unwelcome or are barred from participating in certain business arenas due to their economic standing, this represents an incomplete form of justice. One might assume that policies are in place to guarantee social justice within the realm of business activities in South Africa. However, instances of exclusion persist, leading Black individuals to feel that they continue to lag economically.

This necessitates a transformation agenda policy implementation that considers racial balance (April & Govender, 2022). As existing research has indicated, the expansion of businesses can also be influenced by the choices and actions of individuals (Wuebker et al. 2015). For instance, the personal decision to pursue education or acquire technical skills, including capitalising on available empowerment opportunities, extends beyond the direct scope of policy interventions. In other words, achieving social justice cannot be solely mandated, particularly when existing policies aim to establish its conditions. Literature shows an imbalance in transformation policies and their approach to getting social justice for a particular group of people in South Africa (Mudau, 2022). This perceived imbalance, evident for over three decades, lies in the pronounced and consistent emphasis on Black South Africans. To phrase it differently, while sometimes subtle, policies often make it clear that more opportunities are and will be directed towards Black South Africans, with a particular focus on women, since inclusivity is a fundamental aspect of social justice. The argument is that the policy exhibits an imbalance and might inadvertently exclude and overlook the nation's diversity since 1994. Alternative approaches may exist to reorient such policies towards achieving more comprehensive social justice and inclusion (Sisk, 2017). The tensions observed within the business sector and the recurring conflicts surrounding opportunities, especially in the agricultural and mining industries, can be attributed to policies that are perceived as imbalanced.

Several nations share similarities with South Africa regarding their diverse populations and pursuit of transformative agendas. Examples of multicultural societies grappling with similar issues include Australia, Canada, the United Kingdom, and even the United States (Metz et al. 2016). These countries frequently acknowledge their history of settling on lands traditionally belonging to aboriginal or indigenous peoples and the resulting loss of opportunities for those communities. While their specific understandings of social justice may vary, there are parallels in their approaches to ensuring fairness and demonstrating a commitment to equality for all, particularly for groups who have historically experienced disadvantage. A common element in their policies is the provision of opportunities for education and business success. These transformation policies often aim to offer equal opportunities to everyone, but in some cases, such as in Canada, priority is given to Indigenous populations (Gaudry & Lorenz, 2018). There is often a consistent emphasis on reconciliation and an effort to foster peace within these policies. Consequently, social justice can sometimes be perceived as analogous to sharing a meal from the same plate. However, specific individuals are given the first chance to eat and feel satisfied before others get their share. This is a perspective on social justice held by disadvantaged groups in South Africa and, to some extent, other nations. The ideal scenario would involve equal access for everyone to partake in the meal without denying anyone the right to participate. However, the argument arises that some individuals might consume resources more quickly, or the available resources might not even meet their specific needs, rendering the shared plate concept less effective. This illustrates the challenge governments face: how to provide for the diverse needs of people living within the same country while ensuring that the distribution of resources and opportunities is equal and just.

Multiple nations are actively discussing the most effective methods to ensure social justice, especially regarding allocating social benefits to citizens with varying needs and circumstances (Miller, 2017). Policies often define specific criteria for grant eligibility; however, the rationale for these qualifications is not consistently articulated. The introductory sections of these policies often present the rationale to ensure equity for individuals who have historically faced deprivation. This discussion on justice also encompasses the implications for various population segments and the suitable duration for implementing preferential policies without disadvantaging others. This raises questions on the meaning of social justice and its relevance in other spheres. Politicians often apply the broad definition of social justice in a general sense, seeing it as a tool to boost their appeal by focusing their activities on the majority of the public, who could offer more political support.

In situations where disagreements arise regarding the implementation of social justice, scholarly works often recommend a democratic and inclusive approach to policy deliberation (Miller, 2018). This method is believed to have enhanced and resolved challenges in distributing social benefits in numerous developed nations. This does not suggest that problems will entirely disappear or that there will be no complaints or resistance. Instead, it implies that a collaborative approach to social justice, particularly in business development, could foster knowledge-sharing and lead to policy formulation improvements. This framework is not unfamiliar to the policy consultation processes within South Africa. Evidence indicates that South Africa has dedicated considerable time and resources to developing its policies, intending to ensure that the content of policy documents genuinely reflects the aspirations of the population (Parkhurst, 2017). Nevertheless, the implementation of these policies appears to present ongoing difficulties. The individuals who ultimately receive grants and those who apply for them are frequently from the Black community, highlighting the practical outcomes of the policy in business development. The underlying assumption is that other racial groups or demographics may have benefited from past opportunities, providing them an advantage in achieving business success. Therefore, they may not be the primary target beneficiaries of the current policy's objectives. Some academic perspectives have labelled this outcome as a form of injustice. There is a recognition that not all individuals who have been excluded from receiving grants are necessarily without need. Consequently, there is a requirement to understand better how neoliberal policies may have shaped the perspectives of policymakers (Ban, 2016).

3 Competitive Market and Social Benefits Distribution

The emergence of market-oriented policies, frequently linked to neoliberalism, has heightened competition for social benefits, occasionally requiring government intervention via policy measures. Individuals and entities seek economic opportunities, often through capitalist ventures and the formation of businesses. In this context, governments can effectively dictate who benefits and who may be excluded. In developed nations, governments often impose substantial taxes on highly profitable businesses and influential individuals within specific sectors (Saez & Zucman, 2019). These measures typically allocate generated revenue towards supporting economically disadvantaged citizens or establishing alternative opportunities, including providing free or subsidised education and grants for small business owners. This approach is frequently contested in political campaigns, as politicians often denounce it as inequitable while seeking to gain support by proposing tax reductions for wealthy corporations. Their primary assertion is that all individuals merit an equal opportunity for business success. They argue that imposing significant taxes on profitable companies to support those deemed less fortunate is inherently unjust. From this viewpoint, wealth disparities among individuals or businesses in a competitive market do not inherently render the system unjust. Taxation policies have been extensively debated and frequently criticised for their perceived inequitable effects on successful entrepreneurs (Alston & Reisch, 2019). A significant issue often highlighted is the possibility of tax funds being utilised inefficiently or wastefully, especially if such resources are perceived as mismanaged or unproductively employed. This raises a critical question for governments: How can they ensure fairness in a competitive market while promoting equitable participation and practical contributions from small business owners who need support following assistance? This consideration is particularly pertinent in South Africa, with a substantial demand for robust market performance and social advancement.

Nations that have transitioned from colonial rule, like South Africa, need policies that promote open market systems and healthy competition, supported by a strong tax system (Obeng-Odoom, 2020). As a result, the government is essential in overseeing the economy and safeguarding against exploitation. The rental costs for commercial property in South Africa have significantly increased, correlating with the rise in commodity prices, which major corporations often attribute to the effects of the COVID-19 pandemic. Small businesses, frequently operating under limited grants or facing difficulties securing bank loans, are particularly vulnerable. Studies show that many companies did not last more than three months. This situation usually calls for the government to find ways to help struggling small businesses, maybe using policies leveraging resources from more established, more prominent companies. The political parties in power greatly influence the pragmatic nature of these policies by aligning with the wealthy, who would oppose higher taxes. The widening wealth discrepancies clearly show social injustice in line with Keynesian economic ideas that promote government involvement in the market and taxes as measures of redistribution of wealth.

3.1 Keynesian Theory of Wealth Distribution

The towering figure of twentieth-century economic theory, John Maynard Keynes, transformed macroeconomics with his understanding of the forces behind economic activity and the role that government intervention plays (Keynes, 1936). Although his main concentration was on controlling aggregate demand to reach full employment and economic stability, his theories have consequences for wealth distribution, even if they are usually indirectly relevant. Knowing the Keynesian viewpoint on wealth means recognising his divergence from conventional economic ideas and his focus on the interdependence of macroeconomic factors. Knowing Keynesian ideas, primarily through their impact on income creation, asset value, and the function of the state, provides a foundation for understanding and maybe changing the distribution of wealth within a rising economy like South Africa.

Emerging in reaction to the Great Depression, Keynesian economics questioned the conventional wisdom holding that markets would inevitably self-regulate to reach full employment. According to Keynes (1936), the main factor influencing an economy's degree of economic activity is its overall demand—that is, total expenditure in that system. Regardless of flexible salaries and prices, insufficient overall demand could result in extended recession and unemployment. His solution was vigorous government intervention through fiscal policy, changing government expenditure and taxation to boost demand during recessionary times. Although Keynes' immediate focus was not the distribution of current wealth, the protracted periods of high unemployment and economic misery during the Depression surely underlined the social and economic effects of concentrated wealth and great poverty (Skidelsky, 2003).

The idea of the multiplier effect—that an initial government expenditure injection into the economy results in a more significant general increase in economic activity—is fundamental to Keynesian theory (Keynes, 1936). This happens because the initial expenditure produces revenue for people and businesses, who then spend some of it to generate more income and consumption. This process keeps on increasing the initial impact even though the rewards are declining. Within the framework of wealth, driven by efficient demand management, steady periods of economic development and full employment might present more chances for wealth generation in many spheres of life. However, at different rates, more people are saving and accumulating assets when more people are working, and earnings are rising.

Moreover, Keynesian theory stresses the part expectations play in guiding investment decisions (Keynes, 1936). Even with low lending rates, businesses could be reluctant to make investments in uncertain and low-confidence periods. Government intervention can help increase business confidence and inspire investment by offering a consistent economic environment and raising aggregate demand—more investment results in building new capital assets—a fundamental component of national prosperity. Although the ownership of these assets may first be concentrated, by giving more people the capacity to buy assets, the resulting economic growth and employment creation might indirectly help progressively distribute wealth over time.

Although Keynes did not specifically create a thorough theory of wealth distribution, his focus on the government's role in controlling the economy has major ramifications for how money is gathered and distributed. Though these were not necessarily Keynes' main goals, fiscal policy's main instrument in his toolkit can affect wealth distribution via several channels.

The keystone of many contemporary fiscal systems shaped by Keynesian ideas is that progressive taxation can help redistribute wealth (Atkinson, 2015). Although Keynes himself concentrated more on the use of taxation to control aggregate demand, the notion of taxing higher incomes and maybe wealth at higher rates can, over time, help to lower the concentration of wealth at the top (Piketty, 2014). Public services, including healthcare and education, which benefit all members of society, even those with lower incomes and fewer assets, can then be funded from the funds created by progressive taxation. This can be considered a kind of social wealth creation since it gives less wealthy people access to necessary services that might otherwise demand large personal expenditures, indirectly boosting their general well-being and possible upward mobility capacity.

Furthermore, affecting wealth distribution is government expenditure on infrastructure projects, including public transportation, bridges, and road building. These expenditures generate long-term assets that help the whole economy in addition to short-term increases in demand. Better infrastructure can increase production, lower transportation costs, and provide chances for companies and people in different areas, possibly resulting in a more geographically scattered distribution of economic activity and wealth generation.

Moreover, Keynesian theory recognises the possibility of market shortcomings and the need for government action to fix them (Keynes, 1936). Regarding the distribution of wealth, this could support laws meant to control financial markets to stop too strong speculation and the creation of asset bubbles disproportionately favouring the rich (Minsky, 1986). Although Keynes personally paid less attention to financial control than contemporary economists have, his stress on the volatility of markets and the requirement of government supervision provide a theoretical basis for such measures.

Although Keynes' main concern was fiscal policy, monetary policy—run by central banks—also significantly affects economic activity and wealth distribution inside a Keynesian framework. Monetary policy tools, such as changing interest rates and managing the money supply, can influence asset values and produce wealth impacts that vary and affect different groups of people.

Common monetary policy reaction to boost economic activity during recessions—lowering interest rates—may cause asset prices, especially equities and homes, to rise. This is so because reduced borrowing costs help companies and people fund asset purchases, therefore stimulating demand and raising prices. Although this helps asset holders, who are usually wealthier (Piketty, 2014), it can also make it more difficult for those with limited assets to join the market, aggravating wealth disparity.

On the other hand, if utilised to fight inflation, higher interest rates could have a reverse impact and perhaps lower asset values. Therefore, depending on their asset levels and financial status, the effect of monetary policy on wealth distribution is complicated and can have both good and negative results for different groups.

In financial markets, Keynesian economics also emphasises the need to control expectations (Keynes, 1936). Particularly for highly leveraged people, irrational exuberance and speculative bubbles can cause unsustainable rises in asset prices followed by violent crashes that can wipe out large volumes of wealth (Minsky, 1986). Although Keynes lacked a fully developed theory of asset bubbles, his focus on the part psychological elements play in influencing investment decisions set the foundation for later work in behavioural economics and financial market instability, directly relevant to the knowledge of wealth concentration and its volatility.

Although Keynes' direct attention to wealth distribution was restricted, later economists expanded and modified his fundamental theories to handle problems of inequality. For instance, post-Keynesian economists have focused more on how institutions, power dynamics, and historical events shape both income and wealth distribution (Palley, 2012). They contend that social conventions, political systems, and collective negotiating strength all affect the way wealth is distributed in addition to market pressures.

From a Keynesian point of view, another important factor is the interaction between income and wealth inequalities (Galbraith, 1998.). Although Keynes concentrated mostly on controlling aggregate demand to reach full employment and stable prices, prolonged high-income inequality can negatively affect collective demand. Underconsumption and slowed economic development can result from a significant amount of income accumulating in a small segment of the population with a stronger tendency to save. In contrast, the majority of the population has limited disposable income. For most, this underconsumption can restrict chances for wealth building.

Keynesian concepts are still pertinent in modern arguments on wealth distribution. The emphasis on government intervention to stabilise the economy and promote full employment can be seen as a necessary condition for creating broader opportunities for wealth creation. Programmes for education and job training, among other fiscal policies meant to be investments in human capital, can help raise lower-income people's earning potential, thereby enhancing their capacity to save and build assets over time (Atkinson, 2015).

Furthermore, the Keynesian concern with aggregate demand and the potential for underconsumption in highly unequal societies provides a rationale for policies that aim to reduce income inequality, such as progressive taxation and stronger social safety nets (Piketty, 2014). These policies can help to sustain aggregate demand and build a more stable and inclusive economy where the advantages of economic growth are more generally shared, indirectly leading to a more fair distribution of wealth over the long run by increasing the disposable income of lower and middle-income households.

While John M. Keynes did not develop a specific theory of wealth distribution, his ground-breaking work on macroeconomics has significant, albeit often indirect, implications for understanding and influencing how wealth is distributed within an economy. His emphasis on the active role of government in managing aggregate demand to achieve full employment and economic stability provides a foundation for broader opportunities for wealth creation across different segments of society (Keynes, 1936). Fiscal policies influenced by Keynesian principles, such as progressive taxation and government spending on public goods and infrastructure, can contribute to a more equitable distribution of wealth over time (Atkinson, 2015). While primarily focused on price stability and full employment, monetary policy can also significantly affect asset valuations and wealth (Minsky, 1986).

The extensions of Keynesian thought by subsequent economists, particularly in the post-Keynesian tradition, have further highlighted the complex interplay between macroeconomic policies, income inequality, and wealth distribution (Palley, 2012). The modern relevance of Keynesian ideas stems from their capacity to guide policy discussions meant to produce a more stable, inclusive, and fair economy where the advantages of economic growth are more generally shared, thus reducing the concentration of wealth (Piketty, 2014). While Keynesian economics may not offer a direct blueprint for wealth redistribution, its focus on managing the macroeconomy and the role of the state provides a crucial framework for understanding the indirect pathways through which wealth distribution can be influenced and improved.

Expanding on the influence of Keynesian principles on wealth distribution at a macroeconomic level, it is essential to analyse the specific context of small and medium-sized enterprises (SMEs) in South Africa, with a focus on the performance of Black-owned businesses. The challenges identified above, including underperformance relative to other groups and the complexities of grant funding, can be further elucidated by examining the broader Keynesian concepts of aggregate demand, access to capital, and the role of government intervention as they pertain to this vital sector of the South African economy. The current discussion can assist in analysing how a Keynesian perspective may guide strategies to enhance growth and improve the performance of Black-owned SMEs in South Africa.

Hence, Keynesian economic thought implies that government intervention in the market is crucial in redistributing wealth throughout society (Seccareccia & Lavoie, 2016). However, a potentially overlooked aspect of this argument is the principle of social justice in how wealth is distributed. Still, in the twenty-first century, especially in South Africa, economic policy cannot afford to ignore the critical issue of inequality and the need for government involvement. Simultaneously, it is unlikely that wealth distribution motivated only by political advantage will promote actual growth. This is evident in how grants have been allocated to small and medium-sized enterprises (SMEs), a practice that scholarly work has identified as a policy injustice (Govender, 2019). Put differently, government intervention, such as collecting taxes from large corporations to support small businesses, should ideally lead to tangible and positive outcomes. This critical element seems to be missing in the current strategies for financing SMEs in South Africa.

Based on Keynesian theory, the ability to earn and spend money is important as consumption and production contribute to efficiency in a country. Production can be encouraged when the South African government encourages SMEs to create innovative products rather than relying on importation. Nonetheless, overarching economic conditions substantially affect the adequacy of earnings and the employment status of individuals. Employment produces income, which may then be allocated to savings or expenditure. Thus, controlling the labour market is vital to safeguard workers from exploitation, while managing inflation is another critical element influencing decisions regarding saving versus spending. In South Africa, inflation and employment rates have compelled households to prioritise spending on essential consumer goods. Keynes' fundamental work, 'The General Theory of Employment, Interest and Money', released in 1936, provides a profound study of modern economics, particularly demonstrating how unchecked inflation can adversely affect total economic production. Strategically financing SMEs in South Africa constitutes an innovative and economically viable strategy. Nonetheless, the achievement of comprehensive macroeconomic development depends on consumer income levels and their willingness to spend. Keynes championed measures designed to augment income, as this directly affects consumption (shown by the equation $C = m + nY$, where C represents consumption spending and Y indicates national income, inclusive of taxes). Considering that SMEs rely on consumer purchasing decisions, it is imperative to examine consumer behaviour trends concerning inflation over the past thirty years since South Africa's democratic transition to accurately evaluate the impact and efficacy of government grants.

As a result, government funding policies should ideally take an output-oriented strategy, focusing on tangible outcomes rather than simply giving funding as inputs for change or correcting inequities. From a social justice perspective, taxpayers who contribute a more significant share of the funds used by the government to help small enterprises may see the current system as unfair unless it produces demonstrable positive results. A key question arises: How many small businesses, having received investment since 1994, have effectively grown to become mega organisations, paying considerably through taxes and employing others who also contribute to the tax base? This type of growth would reflect a tangible form of social justice in funding, aligning with the expectations of those who donate the most money. Suppose the government views large, high-tax-paying enterprises solely as a means to a goal. In that case, merely a source of funding to help others—the significant expansion of small businesses in South Africa will likely remain a distant possibility for some time.

4 Linearity of Framing Social Justice in Business Value Creation

The conceptualisation of social justice and funding for SMEs in South Africa often follows a relatively straightforward, linear pattern. The government prioritises the demands of the majority, who may threaten to withdraw their electoral support if not provided with certain social benefits, potentially at the cost of the small business sector that could ultimately generate these benefits. This simplistic, linear approach to social justice likely contributes to policy shortcomings and the sluggish growth of small businesses in South Africa. What is needed is a comprehensive framework that incorporates accountability for the allocation and utilisation of funds within the policy for recipients (Rungani & Potgieter, 2018). Under such a system, it would be fair to utilise revenue from taxes to assist SMEs in growing their businesses and helping the economy flourish. Likewise, it would be reasonable to know that SMEs effectively use these funds, especially for big companies that pay more taxes. Still, the most important question is determining who is in charge of ensuring funding is spent wisely so that participants can accept that the process is fair and justifiable.

To effectively justify the social justice dimension of funding, small and medium-sized enterprises (SMEs) must develop a business model that produces measurable value for the enterprise and its customers. This value must be precisely defined from the target customers' perspective, representing the first stage of business growth. Additionally, resources designated for SMEs must be utilised strategically to create value, especially in the supply chain and distribution of their products or services. Small and medium-sized enterprises (SMEs) must effectively communicate their value proposition and consistently pursue its realisation until tangible outcomes are achieved (Sinkovics, Hoque & Czaban, 2015). In the context of social justice, the government should actively monitor or clearly outline monitoring strategies within its policy as the provider of SME funding. Small businesses are unlikely to successfully develop and implement a compelling value proposition without access to technical assistance and guidance. Numerous large corporations attain growth due to foundational business knowledge or familial support, which facilitates their mastery of the complexities of business development for success. A well-defined strategy is essential for the success of any business. Consequently, a relevant inquiry emerges: Is it equitable to allocate funding to SMEs without concurrently facilitating their strategic development and capacity to create substantial value from the invested capital?

A crucial element of a blue ocean strategy centres on value creation (Hammer, 2022). Regardless of scale, every business should strive to generate value, which should typically be clearly articulated within its vision and mission statements. A clearly stated vision and mission should enable the government and the relevant funding committees to understand how the business intends to contribute to the broader economic system and evaluate whether its proposed value proposition justifies allocating a specific amount of funding. The criteria for granting financial assistance to SMEs should be based on justice principles, such as whether the business actively contributes to environmental sustainability, fosters skill development, and/or promotes regional development. Furthermore, the individuals or team in charge of administering the firm should clearly describe how the requested cash will be used. Awarding considerable financing to a team with no verifiable business management experience or a bad financial stewardship track record would be unfair.

The expectation is that businesses established with financial support will stimulate development within the entrepreneur's region. In urban centres like Johannesburg and Pretoria, larger businesses tend to dominate, while smaller enterprises are often owned by individuals from White communities or by immigrants. Consequently, there is a pressing need for an increase in businesses owned and operated by Black South Africans, a matter of social justice that policy can now prioritise, marking three decades since the significant societal shifts of the post-apartheid era (see Chimucheka, Muchineripi & Chinyamurindi, 2019). The critical question then becomes how subsequent funding can effectively monitor the growth of these businesses and foster increased economic activity for local populations. The principles of a free market and competition extend beyond mere taxation; they also encompass empowering citizens to actively participate in and benefit from the business opportunities available within the country. It would be advisable for the government to investigate the reasons behind some citizens' reluctance to venture into business beyond the issue of access to funding. It is recommended that entrepreneurial education within both basic and higher education curricula be emphasised to encourage particularly educated young people to consider establishing their businesses upon graduation. Providing funding and support for initiatives that enhance graduate employability and promote entrepreneurial activities is a matter of social justice.

The financial results of funding small and medium-sized enterprises (SMEs) are important markers for determining the efficacy of their operations (Xiang & Worthington, 2017). This mainly refers to the return on financial resources invested or granted by the government to these firms. Although the government does not expect direct repayment of the financing, there is hope that the value these businesses should have earned will indicate their potential for future growth. Beyond monetary gains, SMEs are expected to add non-monetary value, which includes doing business responsibly and cultivating constructive connections with stakeholders in the broader business community. This non-financial value benefits other elements of the business, ultimately adding to profitability and growth, as seen by more significant turnover over time. In contrast, negative feedback can significantly impede a company's success, which emphasises the value of soft skills for SMEs, as negative feedback can harm their reputation and restrict their growth trajectory. SMEs have a social duty and are accountable to taxpayers, whose contributions allow the government to adopt social subsidies or funding interventions. As a result, the value these enterprises provide, both financial and non-financial, directly influences the social fairness of taxpayer money spent. Finally, SMEs must create excellent customer experiences to ensure their long-term viability and present an apparent reason for the financial assistance they have received.

The distribution of funding by government entities and the application of these resources by small and medium-sized enterprises (SMEs) in some sectors often lead to an implicit framework that influences business practices. In South Africa, various government regulatory authorities oversee business operations, including issuing necessary permits for enterprises offering sensitive services, particularly in the healthcare sector, as all enterprises, irrespective of size, must adhere to regulations. Smaller businesses that meet designated profit thresholds may be exempt from certain taxes; however, they must still adhere to other mandatory requirements based on the nature of their operations. Competition is a consistent factor, particularly in profitable and lucrative business sectors. As a result, sustainable growth and a positive market reputation will only be achievable by businesses that consistently adhere to government regulations and operate within the legal framework. Non-compliance with these regulations or an inability to access critical information regarding compliance requirements are frequently the reasons for the failure of specific SMEs. This emphasises a substantial area in which policy can provide additional assistance to SMEs to guarantee their sustainability and, in the end, substantiate the use of grant funding.

Another major factor altering the economic landscape is the rapid growth of technology and artificial intelligence (AI). Traditional brick-and-mortar stores are expected to become less common as businesses and customers prefer online transactions to in-person shopping experiences. Nonetheless, technology is expensive, and many small businesses cannot afford to develop a website to market their business adequately. While technology provides opportunities, social media and other technology can expose small businesses to cyber-attacks, resulting in significant financial loss. Notwithstanding these risks, technology continues to be a crucial element of corporate success. In response, the South African government has prioritised a business-oriented digital transformation policy. A significant challenge for policymakers is ensuring equitable access to technology for all enterprises, especially smaller ones. This issue requires meticulous examination to foster the growth and sustainability of small firms in the evolving digital era.

5 The Performance of Funded Small Business

A review of the potential for growth among small enterprises in South Africa revealed a trend of underperformance among companies owned by Black individuals in various provinces. Notably, since 1994, net profit growth for White-owned enterprises has been significantly larger than that of Black African-owned businesses. This gap may indicate that Black-owned businesses experience much higher operating expenses that they struggle to manage or, more broadly, that SMEs are not efficiently regulating their operational costs. Similarly, small enterprises appear to have limited experience in efficient asset management to create profits. As a result, rivals, notably migrant entrepreneurs, have used these market dynamics to grow their enterprises, often with little or no access to official investment. The growing number of small businesses owned by foreign nationals indicates opportunities for collaboration, particularly in other African markets, for Black-owned companies that are currently underperforming. Such partnerships could include mutual learning and resource pooling to create larger, more robust organisations capable of delivering value for their respective industries.

In the last thirty years, small businesses supported by grants have exhibited lower gross profit margins than those with little or no grant funding. Current trends indicate that this disparity is unlikely to diminish without substantial intervention. Businesses with minimal or no government support generally exhibit higher overall gross profits. Businesses dependent on grants may experience lower sales revenue in relation to operational costs, which could be due to insufficient experience in effective business management. A contributing factor may be that grant funding generally does not necessitate repayment, potentially resulting in less rigorous resource management and sales initiatives.

Likewise, an analysis of small businesses and grant beneficiaries in the provinces of South Africa indicates a consistent pattern in business performance, with the notable exceptions of Gauteng and KwaZulu-Natal. This data indicates a potential for the government to realign its policies to support rural communities better, emphasising the development of capacity to create value for local businesses and the communities they serve. It is observed that a limited number of small businesses successfully secure additional financing from banks at low interest rates, and those that do often fail to achieve significant growth with the extra capital. This indicates that financial support alone is insufficient to address the challenges encountered by emerging businesses. A significant deficiency in essential business skills is evident among small or new business owners nationwide.

A key priority for numerous small business owners looking for funding appears to be the expansion and development of their ventures. Consequently, they must clearly understand the competitive landscape, particularly the presence of larger, more established businesses within their operating locations. The value of a small business' non-current assets can often serve as a reliable indicator of its overall financial worth in South Africa. This information holds significant value when deciding on the most appropriate business structure, such as forming a partnership or operating as a sole proprietorship, where the responsibility for decisions and finances rests with a single individual. For numerous small businesses, a significant competitive advantage lies in the wealth of opportunities that remain largely unexplored across various sectors within South Africa.

Consequently, the South African government may benefit from actively encouraging increased collaboration among businesses, wherein multiple enterprises combine their innovative ideas and resources to improve their likelihood of success. This business model may pose challenges concerning governance and leadership; however, it can significantly enhance business development in the country, contingent upon the implementation of robust and effective policies governing such collaborations. Many small business owners function autonomously, making all business decisions independently and thus bearing the full risk of potential venture failure. Adopting business collaboration requires a transformation in the management and leadership frameworks of the involved organisations. The potential benefits for partners are considerable, encompassing the exchange of valuable technology and diverse skills, which may result in significant growth or the capacity to capture larger market segments. In business combinations or collaborations, all parties must comprehend risk management and employ transfer, avoidance, reduction, or acceptance strategies. Collective decision-making significantly enhances the likelihood of business success, particularly when analysing historical performance data that suggests sole proprietorships typically experience lower success rates over time.

6 Concluding Remarks: Towards an Equitable and Efficient Framework for SMEs' Support in South Africa

Examining social justice within the intricate fabric of post-apartheid policies—more especially, those meant to encourage and develop Black-owned enterprises in South Africa—exposes a profoundly entwined and sometimes controversial interaction of political, economic, and social elements. These elements still greatly affect the course of continuous national growth as well as the quest for a fairer society. Though marked by admirable intentions, South Africa's path to redress the deep-seated historical injustices and systematic inequalities caused by the repressive apartheid government mostly through transforming projects like Black Economic Empowerment (BEE) and strategically targeted SME funding programmes, so attesting to the nation's will to change. Notwithstanding the significant progress made, the nation still struggles with ongoing, often profoundly ingrained issues that impede the whole and effective implementation of its ambitious goals for economic empowerment, social justice, and tangible equity. Particularly during times of economic crisis, global disturbance, or major societal upheaval, such as the recent COVID-19 pandemic, the data presented in this analysis points to a possible disconnection and, at times, even a palpable confusion in the practical application of the fundamental concepts of equity and equality inside the design and implementation of funding initiatives. This continuous battle to balance conflicting interests and attain concrete results emphasises the crucial and immediate requirement of a forward-looking viewpoint that transcends mere identification of the issues and acceptance of historical flaws. Moving boldly beyond only noting the difficulties and starting to develop innovative ideas and techniques that will greatly improve the general efficacy as well as the important social justice aspects of SME support in South Africa is vital.

The delicate and often unstable balance that policymakers must strike is a core tension consistently and powerfully emphasised throughout this debate. This entails guaranteeing the fair distribution of economic opportunities, resources, and benefits to all spheres of South African society, especially those that have been historically underprivileged and excluded, while simultaneously promoting sustainable and strong overall economic growth. Although government policies have, understandably and justifiably, given Black South Africans a strong and consistent emphasis on addressing the residual and often profoundly ingrained effects of past injustices and systematic imbalances, there is a growing and increasingly urgent awareness that a more complex, sophisticated, and ultimately sustainable approach is now required. This change in strategic thinking and policy development would assist in preventing the unexpected result of unintentionally excluding, ignoring, or marginalising other groups within the very diverse population of the country. The ultimate aim is to move forcefully toward the development of an inclusive and equitable economic environment in which every citizen, regardless of their racial, social, or economic background, is allowed to participate fully, contribute meaningfully, and finally prosper. Such a basic paradigm change in policy orientation calls for a break from what may be defined as a more linear, simplified, and maybe limited knowledge of social justice. Rather, there must be a strong and relentless dedication to accepting a more holistic, comprehensive, and finally transforming framework that recognises, respects, and efficiently addresses the several needs, varied aspirations, and significant potential contributions of every person living in South African society.

Several important areas deserve thoughtful, targeted, consistent, and immediate attention by policymakers, corporate leaders, civil society organisations, and other stakeholders dedicated to creating a fair and equitable future for South Africa to achieve these ambitious but vital aspirations properly. First, above all else, improving and strengthening current policy frameworks is vital. Policies must be painstakingly developed, carefully carried out, strictly enforced, routinely reviewed, and updated to guarantee that they effectively promote equitable access to funding, resources, and a wide range of support mechanisms for all entrepreneurs, regardless of background, while simultaneously addressing the residual and sometimes firmly rooted consequences of historical disadvantage and systematic discrimination. Establishing clear, transparent, and simply understandable eligibility requirements for grant programmes, loan schemes, and other financial assistance calls for a strong and relentless dedication. Moreover, there must be a relentless commitment to guarantee the best degrees of openness, responsibility, and moral behaviour throughout the allocation process—from the first application stage to the last fund distribution and the following monitoring and assessment of their use. Not only are these clarity, openness, and responsibility desirable, but they are necessary for developing and preserving trust among all stakeholders, promoting a strong sense of justice and legitimacy in the support system, and, finally, ensuring that public resources are used effectively and efficiently to accomplish their intended use.

Though vital and required, the provision of financial aid represents only one piece of a much more complicated and linked puzzle, so it is imperative to acknowledge and stress this fact. Apart from providing funding to budding entrepreneurs, SMEs—especially Black-owned businesses—should get a complete, all-encompassing package of assistance tools. These support systems must be strategically planned, meticulously executed, and constantly changed to meet the broad spectrum of linked problems these companies usually face in pursuing long-term sustainability, significant expansion, and efficient involvement in the larger economy. This covers but is most definitely not limited to, a strong and continuous focus on skill improvement. Empowering entrepreneurs with the knowledge, skills, and expertise required to properly run their companies, increase their financial literacy and access to capital, and leverage the transforming power of technology to enhance their operations, streamline their processes, and widen their market reach calls for giving access to high-quality training and mentorship programmes.

Another vital element of a strong and efficient support system is enabling access to markets inside South Africa and in the progressively linked global arena while concurrently promoting a level playing field, guaranteeing fair competition, and preventing anti-competitive practices. This could entail the implementation of focused initiatives that link SMEs to bigger, more established supply chains, support their participation in important trade fairs, exhibitions, and networking events, and actively address any anti-competitive practices, such as predatory pricing or market manipulation, that may unfairly hinder their progress, limit their growth potential, and prevent them from totally engaging in the economy. Moreover, strategic infrastructure development is essential and sometimes unappreciated in producing an environment fit for sustainable corporate development and economic success. Particularly in rural communities and historically underdeveloped areas, where the demand for such resources is often highest, this calls for focused and consistent investments in the development and maintenance of dependable transportation networks, the provision of consistent access to basic utilities, including electricity, water, and internet connectivity, and the establishment of well-equipped business parks, incubation centres, and other support facilities.

Effective adoption and use of technology is now an absolute need for survival, competitiveness, and long-term success in the fast-changing, increasingly linked, and very competitive digital age that we live in. It is not a luxury for companies of any kind. Therefore, it is imperative to actively assist SMEs in adopting and smoothly including digital technology in their primary company processes. This help should be all-encompassing, covering technical knowledge and continuous support as well as training and financial aid through subsidies or incentives. The aim is to empower SMEs to increase their operational efficiency, simplify their procedures, reach their market outside geographical constraints, and equip them with the knowledge, tools, and resources required to properly minimise the always-existing dangers of cyber-attacks, data breaches, and other digital threats.

Encouragement of strategic alliances and teamwork offers another effective but sometimes underused means of supporting SMEs' expansion, creativity, and long-term survival. Actively supporting and enabling cooperative projects among companies, including creating strategic alliances between established, successful companies and developing SMEs, can help maximise the pooling of resources, enable the development of more creative and innovative market expansion strategies, and help facilitate priceless knowledge-sharing. Black-owned businesses especially stand to gain from this cooperative approach since it gives them access to resources, networks, and knowledge that will enable them to achieve economies of scale, improve their competitiveness, and successfully compete in bigger, more competitive markets, both domestically and abroad.

Any SME's success depends on the creation of strong, open, and accountable systems for evaluating influence and guaranteeing appropriate public fund use. Tracking the success of funding projects, evaluating their impact on the ground, and ensuring the appropriate and effective use of public money depend on strict monitoring and evaluation procedures being indispensable. Such steps entail analysing the more considerable social and economic value produced by the companies that get support in addition to the direct financial returns on investment—such as higher income, profitability, or job creation. Such a thorough and all-encompassing assessment system will enable legislators to make data-driven decisions, maximise their strategies for maximum impact, and guarantee that public resources are used effectively and efficiently to attain the intended outcomes while supporting openness and responsibility.

Lastly, and maybe most importantly, we must encourage a dynamic, inclusive entrepreneurial culture across South Africa, which involves establishing a conducive and empowering atmosphere that actively supports innovation, welcomes measured risk-taking, and advances business development as a realistic and desired career path for every citizen, from all backgrounds. This transforming cultural change calls for a multifarious, long-term strategy. Education is crucial; thus, including entrepreneurial education in curricula and higher education programmes is crucial to equip the next generations with the skills, knowledge, and entrepreneurial attitude required to succeed in the demanding and competitive corporate environment. By highlighting successful Black entrepreneurs as positive role models, one may challenge current preconceptions and show that success is possible regardless of background, therefore inspiring and motivating aspirant business owners. Furthermore, it is imperative to aggressively remove the systematic obstacles that discourage or impede entrepreneurship, including limited access to reasonably priced finance, demanding regulations, and firmly rooted social prejudices that might unfairly disadvantage or discourage particular groups or people from following their entrepreneurial aspirations.

Finally, South Africa can make major and long-lasting progress toward creating a just, equitable, and far more effective framework for supporting SMEs' sustainable development and expansion by embracing these recommendations and following a comprehensive, integrated, and forward-looking strategy. This revolutionary change would empower Black entrepreneurs, who have traditionally been excluded and underprivileged from the economic mainstream and release the great and usually unrealised economic potential housed within the varied and active South African population. The outcome will be the development of a richer, more inclusive, and fairer society in which every one of its people has a chance to flourish, significantly help the national economic development, and share in the advantages of the success of their country. It is imperative to recognise that the journey towards achieving true and lasting social justice is an ongoing and evolving process, one that demands continuous adaptation, open and honest dialogue, and an unwavering commitment from all stakeholders to building a business environment where every individual, regardless of their background, has the opportunity to succeed, prosper, and contribute meaningfully to the growth, development, and overall progress of South Africa.

References

Alston, P., & Reisch, N. (Eds.). (2019). *Tax, inequality, and human rights*. Oxford University Press.

April, R. A., & Govender, C. M. (2022). Understanding affirmative action leadership in the south African financial context. *African Journal of Business Management, 16*(5), 90–103.

Atkinson, A. B. (2015). *Inequality: What can be done?* Harvard University Press.

Ban, C. (2016). *Ruling ideas: How global neoliberalism goes local*. Oxford University Press.

Boudreaux, K. (2010). Land reform as social justice: The case of South Africa. *Economic Affairs, 30*(1), 13–20.

Chimucheka, T., Muchineripi, J., & Chinyamurindi, W. (2019). A narrative analysis of barriers encountered by a sample of immigrant entrepreneurs in the eastern cape province of South Africa. *TD: The Journal for Transdisciplinary Research in Southern Africa, 15*(1), 1–9.

Galbraith, J. K. (1998). *Created unequal: The crisis in American pay*. Twentieth Century Fund.

Gaudry, A., & Lorenz, D. (2018). Indigenization as inclusion, reconciliation, and decolonization: Navigating the different visions for indigenizing the Canadian academy. *AlterNative: An International Journal of Indigenous Peoples, 14*(3), 218–227.

Goga, S., Bosiu, T., & Bell, J. (2019). Linking IDC finance to structural transformation and inclusivity in post-apartheid South Africa. *Development Southern Africa, 36*(6), 821–838.

Govender, D. (2019). *Economic empowerment through business loans-a critical look at credit protection law for small, micro and medium enterprises in South Africa and Australia* (doctoral dissertation).

Graafland, J. (2019). Economic freedom and corporate environmental responsibility: The role of small government and freedom from government regulation. *Journal of Cleaner Production, 218*, 250–258.

Hammer, T. (2022). Value innovation by creating blue oceans. *Open access. Library Journal, 9*.

Hassen, E. K. G. M. (2018). *The political economy of government spending on small business and entrepreneurship in South Africa* (doctoral dissertation).

Juggernath, S. (2019). *Strategies, challenges and best practices in implementing black economic empowerment in selected south African companies* (doctoral dissertation).

Keynes, J. M. (1936). *The general theory of employment, interest and money*. Macmillan.

Makgoba, M. (2024). Reproduction and communication of apartheid relations of power through the discourses of black economic empowerment in South Africa. *Cogent Arts & Humanities, 11*(1), 2396646.

Metz, I., Ng, E. S., Cornelius, N., Hoobler, J. M., & Nkomo, S. (2016). A comparative review of multiculturalism in Australia, Canada, the United Kingdom, the United States and South Africa. In *research handbook of international and comparative perspectives on diversity management* (pp. 131-170).

Miller, D. (2017). Distributive justice: What the people think. In *Distributive justice* (pp. 135–173). Routledge.

Miller, D. (2018). Is deliberative democracy unfair to disadvantaged groups? In *Democracy as public deliberation* (pp. 201–226). Routledge.

Minsky, H. P. (1986). *Stabilizing an unstable economy*. Yale University Press.

Mudau, D. (2022). *The influence of broad-based black economic empowerment policies on organisational effectiveness: a case of south African companies* (doctoral dissertation).

Obeng-Odoom, F. (2020). The African continental free trade area. *American Journal of Economics and Sociology, 79*(1), 167–197.

Palley, T. I. (2012). *From financial crisis to stagnation: The destruction of shared prosperity and the growth of debt*. Cambridge University Press.

Parkhurst, J. (2017). *The politics of evidence: from evidence-based policy to the good governance of evidence*. Taylor & Francis.

Piketty, T. (2014). *Capital in the twenty-first century*. Belknap Press of Harvard University Press.

Rungani, E. C., & Potgieter, M. (2018). The impact of financial support on the success of small, medium and micro enterprises in the eastern cape province. *Acta Commercii, 18*(1), 1–12.

Saez, E., & Zucman, G. (2019). *The triumph of injustice: How the rich dodge taxes and how to make them pay*. WW Norton & Company.

Seccareccia, M., & Lavoie, M. (2016). Income distribution, rentiers, and their role in a capitalist economy: a Keynes–Pasinetti perspective. *International Journal of Political Economy, 45*(3), 200–223.

Shava, E. (2016). Black economic empowerment in South Africa: Challenges and prospects. *Journal of Economics and Behavioral Studies, 8*(6 (J)), 161–170.

Sisk, T. (2017). *Democratization in South Africa: The elusive social contract* (Vol. 5202). Princeton University Press.

Skidelsky, R. (2003). *John Maynard Keynes: 1883–1946: Economist, philosopher, statesman*. Penguin Books.

Wuebker, R., Hampl, N., & Wuestenhagen, R. (2015). The strength of strong ties in an emerging industry: Experimental evidence of the effects of status hierarchies and personal ties in venture capitalist decision making. *Strategic Entrepreneurship Journal, 9*(2), 167–187.

Xiang, D., & Worthington, A. C. (2017). The impact of government financial assistance on the performance and financing of Australian SMEs. *Accounting Research Journal, 30*(4), 447–464.

CHAPTER 4

Departing from Privileged to Merit-Based Grant Support Programmes

1 Introduction

Many of the small businesses in South Africa are informal. There are 2.6 million SMEs in the country; 15% of business owners operate in rural communities. Only about 37% of small businesses comply with formal regulations and operations. Therefore, measuring the performance of informal businesses is difficult. Yet, performance measurement is essential for policy review purposes. Assessment requires clear guidelines, and literature suggests that evaluation may consider it from a BBBEE perspective (Van Niekerk, 2019). Enwereji et al. (2023) recommended merit-based funding and an effective scoring system to allocate funding for SMMEs during COVID-19. Consequently, there is a correlation between the merit-based approach to funding and the performance of grants (Park & Liang, 2020). Merit-based policies also imply support for businesses regardless of their size, as illustrated in the case of affirmative action for Malaysia and South Africa. In this chapter, the author argues that Malaysia and South Africa have made conscious efforts to implement policies that support disadvantaged groups, such as Bumiputeras and Blacks. This

The original version of the chapter has been revised. A correction to this chapter can be found at
https://doi.org/10.1007/978-981-95-2864-6_7

T. O. Aluko, *Evaluation of Small Business Support in Post-Apartheid South Africa*, https://doi.org/10.1007/978-981-95-2864-6_4

support encompasses access to education and economic opportunities, including employment and business ownership. The number of beneficiaries has significantly increased over time. Regarding capacity development and competitiveness, the author indicates that challenges remain. There is a need to reform the system and focus more on policies and activities supporting individual growth and development, rather than on race. In other words, race-based policies appear to be overly political and disproportionately focused on addressing the issues of a specific ethnic group without thoroughly assessing their impact on the entire population. In the long run, such an approach often seems ineffective and redundant, as the government tends to count the number of beneficiaries without evaluating what those figures indicate in terms of the efficiency of the social programme.

Social programmes must be measured and evaluated in terms of effectiveness and performance. Governments are interested in knowing whether their objectives are achieved through different indicators. Thus, the performance evidence of social programmes often begins with the objective statement. However, some objectives cannot be achieved through quantitative indicators, as they usually require a set of checklists, often referred to as requirements, that applicants must meet for approval of grants. These indicators represent obligatory performance, and entrepreneurs are typically judged according to them. Quantitative performance measurement methods alone are problematic because they cannot convey how the numbers are achieved. The challenges and efforts that contribute to these numbers are often unknown. To improve policies, governments may need to adopt comprehensive evaluations that will allow for the continual improvement of policies. The literature has shown that various countries, particularly in Africa, face challenges in measuring the performance of their social programmes. For instance, the challenges encountered by developing countries, such as Nigeria, are related to implementing policies that support SMEs (Joseph et al., 2021). In this context, implementing policies may be hindered by other systemic issues, including allocating and utilising resources and a lack of accountability. It might be difficult to measure the performance of entrepreneurs as well as the support they receive. However, the issue of policy implementation is a global phenomenon, though it is particularly prevalent in Africa. Research has indicated that developed countries face similar challenges in supporting SMEs, such as a lack of access to good mentors, financial difficulties, and negative bank attitudes towards new business owners, creating barriers. Nonetheless, the findings also demonstrate how certain countries have supported business owners despite these challenges (Fielden et al., 2000). In Kenya, Njue (2021) shows that implementing Jua-kalis empowerment has contributed to the growth of SMEs. This indicates that countries within the developing world can implement successful programmes for entrepreneurs.

Through evaluation, the South African government can identify loopholes in the policy and implementation of social programmes. Therefore, the objectives of grants for SMEs in South Africa after 1994 need to be assessed for their effectiveness and relevance in recent times. This evaluation may encompass the effectiveness of the funding formula, the methodology for distributing grants to SMEs, and whether the programme achieves its stated objectives. Literature suggests that the government should prioritise merit-based programmes, particularly in distributing grants to SMEs, while focusing less on race-based social benefit agendas aimed at inclusivity, diversity, and development. When analysing the performance or effectiveness of social programmes in South Africa, it is crucial to examine factors that might enable SMEs that have not received grants to perform better than those that have received support. This counterfactual factor could necessitate re-evaluating how social benefits are distributed in post-apartheid South Africa. Over the past 30 years, the net growth of SMEs that have benefited from government grants is insignificant compared to those that have not benefited or secured funding through other channels. This may indicate that SMEs, in general, and particularly those business owners with little experience in managing businesses, may have incurred higher operating costs than business owners without funding who possess better business skills or can manage operating costs more effectively.

Financial support for SMEs includes soft loans (Peter et al. 2018); in some cases, it is provided as guaranteed loans. However, when SMEs cannot secure funding, failure is inevitable (Leboea, 2017). In Nigeria, the challenges faced by SMEs in terms of performance, due to difficulties in obtaining finance, are profound (Adebisi et al., 2015). Nevertheless, a study found that measuring the performance of SMEs also employs non-financial indicators (Maduekwe & Kamala, 2016). However, the use of financial performance facilitates a practical assessment of asset utilisation for productivity (Solani, 2020). Return on investment is one indicator that SMEs can use to control costs and achieve good profits for sustainability. A good return also indicates accountability concerning utilising grants from the government or other entities. Generally, it reflects how effectively SMEs can manage assets and finances to generate business profits. Consequently, these performances can be measured, and the results can assist grant providers in understanding the effectiveness and utilisation of funds in achieving their intended purposes. The South African government has social responsibilities to support business owners and is expected to perform this role objectively, considering the specific context. Likewise, grant recipients should utilise the funds to demonstrate their understanding of the programme's objectives. At which stage does misalignment or confusion arise between what the funder seeks and how the recipient perceives it? Evaluations are expected to consider the intentions of funding as outlined in the policy documents and whether strategies to ensure compliance are articulated and comprehended by the recipients of social grants. This evaluation aims to potentially suggest improvements to policy or recommend a review of aspects that have contributed to non-performance. Therefore, the management of social programmes is quite complex. Nonetheless, South Africa and its society would like to determine whether it is economically viable and sustainable to continue financing SMEs, even if they have not yielded the desired results.

The performance margin over the past 30 years is low compared to a group that used other sources of finance to sustain its business. There appears to be strong motivation to drive businesses towards success for those with loan repayments and interest obligations in South Africa. Depending on the magnitude of the financing, the evidence suggests that businesses carefully plan and monitor the use of funds. Therefore, SMEs that are not solely reliant on government support could be more responsible than those business owners who rely on government funding. The discussion surrounding social inequality and the need to redress it requires caution when analysing how individual business owners can use funds to achieve their objectives. In South Africa, the monitoring system for social grants is an area that likely requires close examination. This type of problem is generally a recurring issue in developing countries. It seems these nations intentionally permit corruption but fail to make social programmes effective, creating opportunities for irregularities. A fair assessment of funding year by year is necessary to understand the ratio and deviation in terms of spending and the impact of government funding on supporting SMEs over the past 30 years.

Therefore, economic prosperity achieved through the grants and support provided to small and medium enterprises (SMEs) over time is a viable model for understanding the future. This indicates that SMEs are viewed as agents of sustainable development and are likely to contribute to poverty reduction through their business activities (Abisuga-Oyekunle et al., 2020). However, modelling key performance indicators for business success has posed significant challenges. The modelling of economic implications stemming from funding for SMEs must incorporate linked variables that, if effectively modelled, could forecast economic sustainability for South Africa, for example. There is a tendency to include numerous variables and sometimes indicators that, while related to performance, can introduce complexity. These complexities must be unravelled with data evidence. Consequently, the performance of SMEs is contingent upon whether they receive adequate support and whether such support is designed to promote sustainability (see Prasannath et al., 2024). The crucial point here is to ascertain whether there is a relationship between the type of support provided, SME performance, and economic growth or poverty alleviation. The South African government has been funding SMEs for over three decades and needs to evaluate the success of these interventions (Bushe, 2019). The diverse support mechanisms aim to stimulate economic growth across various sectors. Meanwhile, the efficacy of these supports in enhancing SMEs' activities towards improved performance directly influences economic growth. Performance encompasses transforming businesses in size, revenue, and overall impact. In other words, the government aims to observe how growth in size can lead to revenue generation and, consequently, how it assists in reducing unemployment and poverty in the country (Opute et al., 2022). The manner in which these variables are modelled and analysed is crucial for predicting the impact of grants or support on SME's activities and overall economic performance. Therefore, understanding the context of SMEs in South Africa can provide valuable insight into these issues.

2 Government Grants and Loans Performance

The policy on grants in South Africa is not performance-based. Therefore, the management structure of SMEs is not considered in the grant application process. This management structure should allow an honest assessment of individual business owners' internal quality policies and systems, which may guarantee success when utilising government funds or loans. These performance measurement criteria should inform decisions regarding how business owners recruit staff, manage compensation, handle procurement, and generate profit based on their resources. This structural support is an essential performance indicator for grant funding and a method for evaluating the allocation and utilisation of grants.

It appears that many businesses funded through grants cannot afford advanced technology; however, it is crucial to comprehend the competition posed by larger businesses within their sector. In other words, a business should be able to scan its environment to understand a small company's leadership and governance requirements, including its competitors. This performance indicator can inform grant givers about how a business utilises financial resources and applies business skills to ensure efficient use of funds compared to its competitors. In essence, it indicates that such a business can be trusted with larger funding opportunities if they arise. One way to assess this is by evaluating how businesses make decisions regarding the value of non-current assets, particularly if they wish to partner with or acquire another business. For instance, a failure to grasp this complex issue in acquisitions has led to several businesses' failure within the first few months of their establishment. If this information were made available during the application process to panels determining grant approval, it would provide insights into the business owner's capacity to manage their business competitively.

While businesses are encouraged to partner to raise funds or acquire if their business has accumulated revenue, there should be a model for this because combined leadership and management have their implications. The ability of SME owners to manage their businesses in partnership arrangements can serve as a significant performance indicator for future success when measuring the impact of grants. The most common arrangement for many small businesses in South Africa is to venture into trading as a form of business. This is not considered an innovative start-up. The most important indicator of performance in making grants impactful or resulting in economic development is when governments fund start-ups enabled by technology or technological applications. This approach will shift from a race-based to a merit-based strategy for funding businesses, contributing to the economic success of South Africa. The country will benefit from the technologies and opportunities accompanying this shift. Therefore, it is essential to understand the longitudinal trend of financing businesses through loans. This will help to elucidate the government's efforts and their corresponding effects in terms of performance.

2.1 Trends in Funding Concerning 'Loans' for Small Businesses in South Africa

Literature demonstrates that SMEs in South Africa face several challenges, one of which is the inability to access finance, mainly due to existing policies (Msomi & Olarewaju, 2021). Banking institutions aim to ensure that businesses submitting loan applications can use the funds for profit and repay principal and interest. Consequently, many banks provide checklists for business loan applicants that include collateral requirements, particularly for substantial loan amounts. While obtaining loan approval is crucial for capitalisation, navigating economic turbulence amid rising interest rates and inflation poses another significant challenge for SMEs. The argument is that the government should intervene in financial markets to alleviate burdens placed on financial institutions, especially for small businesses that lack credit records or assets to secure loans. The inability to secure finance is not unique to South Africa; it also affects countries such as Namibia (Baporikar et al., 2016), Ghana (Thompson et al., 2018), and Bangladesh, as well as numerous countries in Asia and the Pacific (Abe et al., 2015). A common factor among these nations is that they are developing countries (see Megersa, 2020), which affects their ability to finance SMEs. While banks fear potential losses due to debt collection issues, the government ensures that banks and small businesses are not exploited while establishing financial relationships.

This policy requires an enabling environment, such as easy market access and growth opportunities for foreign investors. The South African government, however, needs to ensure that foreign direct investment can serve as a means to redirect opportunities and/or utilise revenue from this relationship to increase the budget for small business development. Nonetheless, there is concern that SME owners will struggle, not due to an inability to manage funds effectively, but because of economic challenges that have diminished the population's purchasing power and disposable incomes. Consequently, the government must find ways to ensure SMEs contribute to job creation, poverty reduction, and addressing economic issues. In return, the government should be prepared to provide or increase grants available to SMEs through banks or other channels.

On the other hand, the South African government has increased funding to SMEs, particularly for disadvantaged groups, since 1994, although several issues have arisen surrounding this initiative. Likewise, literature has highlighted the ineffectiveness of allocating funding and its subsequent use. Despite these challenges, the government introduced guaranteed loans to SMEs to supplement initial funding, which was increased during the COVID-19 pandemic. Fig. 1 illustrates a significant increase in government loans in 2011. However, this funding was reduced in 2011 and continued to decrease until 2014. An increase was observed from 2015, persisting through 2017 and during the COVID-19 crisis. The key driver of business success is when SME owners intentionally leverage the funding or loans provided to create employment opportunities in South Africa. This involves making informed decisions about which products and services can be offered to generate profits while also ensuring a positive impact on the South African populace. There is a need to focus the argument on whether SMEs possess the necessary training and experience to make effective business decisions that result in profits and social impact. While business owners may seek funding or loans for business activities, it remains unclear whether policies assess applicants' training and experience as potential factors in utilising the loans or funds to achieve desired results. Research suggests that businesses often fail due to a lack of training and experience. The type of training and the nature of knowledge required by business owners to succeed also play a crucial role, warranting further examination. This implies that the level of education or training of SME owners is vital to understanding how loans or funds can be utilised more effectively.

The increase in government loans to SMEs indicates that the South African government desires to support business development in the country. While this is a positive social policy, guaranteeing loans for SMEs presents specific challenges. Guaranteed loans can diminish the responsibility and accountability of SMEs in the event of business failures or bankruptcies. Evidence in the literature suggests that some business owners, particularly during COVID-19, mismanaged the funds collected for loan guarantees or redirected them for other purposes. This issue may stem from policy shortcomings rather than individual behaviours. The expectation is that the policy concerning loans should have included performance measures regarding using the funds as part of the grant process. The understanding of guarantees has allowed some SMEs to misuse the funds for personal expenses. Therefore, the policy for business development is expected to undergo review and redevelopment in South Africa to ensure clarity of obligations and accountability.

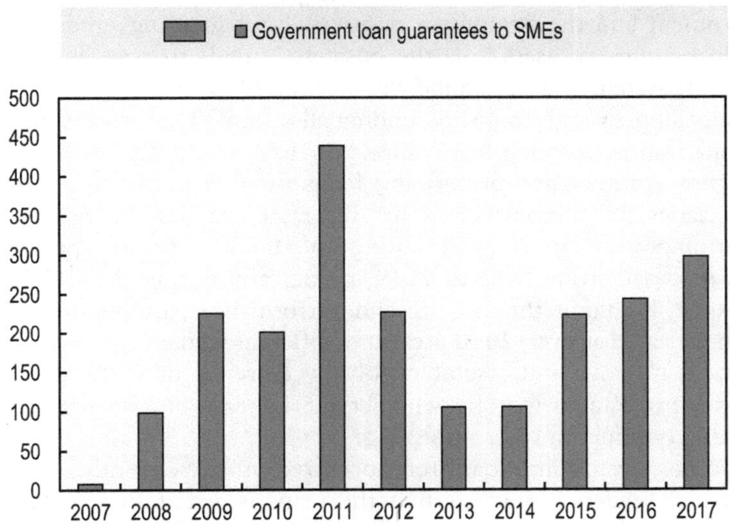

Fig. 1 Government loan guarantees to SMEs Annual, in ZAR million. Source: Financing SMEs and Entrepreneurs 2020. An OECD Scoreboard https://www.oecd.org/en/publications/financing-smes-and-entrepreneurs-2020_061fe03d-en/full-report/component-51.html

Therefore, government funding should be output-based, incorporating an element of accountability, rather than merely providing input-based support to transform or redress inequalities. Within the social justice framework, taxpayers or contributors whose money the government uses to support small businesses may perceive the current approach as unfair unless it results in tangible outputs. In other words, how many small businesses funded since 1994 have successfully scaled into large enterprises that now generate tax revenue and employ individuals who also contribute taxes to the government? This is how accountability in funding will be interpreted and perceived by those who pay taxes. If the government prioritises large businesses that generate significant tax revenue as its primary focus under the assumption that specific individuals require support, developing small businesses in South Africa will remain an elusive goal for an extended period. It is essential for businesses to create value, irrespective of their size. Typically, this value should be clearly articulated in the business' vision and mission statement. Through this statement, the government and the committee responsible for granting funds or loans should be able to assess how the business intends to contribute to the economic system and determine whether the proposed value proposition is compelling enough to justify funding allocation. This process may help mitigate non-performing loans among SMEs.

Figure 2 shows non-performing loans by SMEs. As the number of beneficiaries for business loans has increased, so has the rise in non-performing loans in terms of using the funds. The non-performing loans recorded from 2012 to 2019, particularly during the COVID-19 pandemic, highlight the attitude and performance patterns of SMEs in South Africa. However, 2020 presents a different scenario, as performance began to improve and resembled observed trends of 2009 and 2010. There is no data to indicate whether the increase in loan performance in 2020 continued further into 2024.

The non-performing loan trend occurred more frequently before the pandemic. Evidence suggests that the loans issued during COVID-19 to businesses have demonstrated corresponding performance or assisted entrepreneurs in navigating difficult situations. However, the indicators of this performance are not known. Loan performance is expected to be measured by how the funds are utilised to generate revenue and profit.

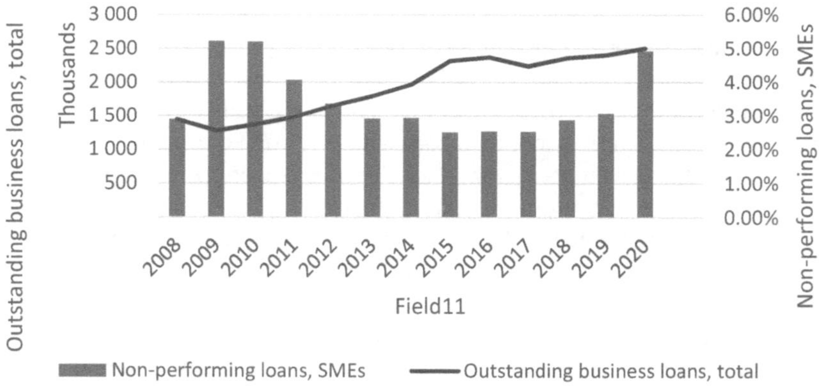

Fig. 2 'Outstanding business loans, total', 'Non-performing loans, SMEs'. Source: Financing SMEs and Entrepreneurs 2020. An OECD Scoreboard—Statlink https://www.oecd.org/en/publications/financing-smes-and-entrepreneurs-2020_061fe03d-en/full-report/component-51.html

Non-performance may necessitate an analysis of sectors and aspects of the economy to identify those that can foster growth in other sectors for overall economic development. There is uneven development in post-apartheid South Africa (Smith et al., 2022). One reason is the excessive focus on industries that have become saturated or possess less potential for local and national economic development. Additionally, the distribution of resources among different sectors and categories of businesses is uneven, creating another form of inequality not only for business owners or beneficiaries but also for many Black communities.

Meanwhile, Fig. 3 provides an understanding of how to measure loan performance in this context. Figure 3 offers a glance at data concerning businesses that have closed or gone bankrupt despite receiving loan financing. There was only an improvement in the businesses that managed to continue from 2009 to 2010. Many businesses struggled and closed between 2011 and 2020. Therefore, the loan performance observed in 2020 is insignificant when examined from a business continuity perspective.

The number of firms or businesses that need rescue, despite guaranteed loans, is increasing, as shown in Fig. 4. The risk factors in managing a business for success, whether internal or external, are profound. Internal

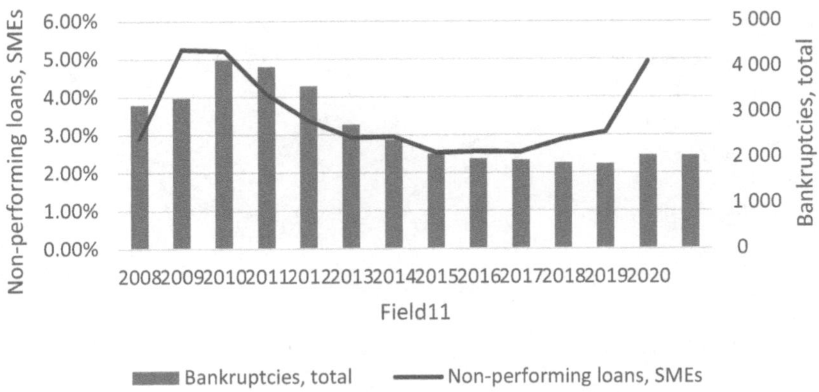

Fig. 3 'Non-performing loans, SMEs', 'Bankruptcies, total' by 'Number of Businesses'. Source: Financing SMEs and Entrepreneurs 2020. An OECD Scoreboard—Statlink https://www.oecd.org/en/publications/financing-smes-and-entrepreneurs-2020_061fe03d-en/full-report/component-51.html

factors may include business owners' socio-demographic backgrounds, which encompass SME owners' training and upbringing. Some studies argue against using demographic characteristics, such as race and gender, as qualifiers or determinants for producing successful SMEs, particularly in South Africa. The premise is that anyone trained, regardless of gender or race, should be able to make an impact when adequately supported or resourced. This argument requires contextual and empirical data to substantiate it. Conversely, external factors will affect all business owners, regardless of gender or race. Government policy concerning taxes and political structures could play a significant role for SMEs, regardless of their business management ability. However, trained SMEs will likely navigate these challenges more effectively than business owners who still require training.

However, the policy surrounding loan allocation is profoundly political and could be enhanced by incorporating merit-based considerations and the country's diversity in the provision of finance. While there appears to be an issue with the utilisation of loans, as evidenced by the number of businesses that have ceased operations, further research is necessary to examine the nature and types of businesses that demonstrate resilience

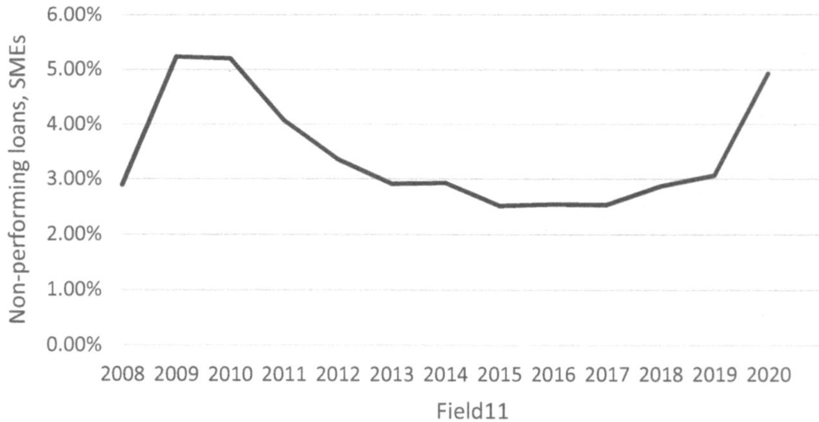

Fig. 4 'Non-performing loans, SMEs'. Source: Financing SMEs and Entrepreneurs 2020. An OECD Scoreboard—Statlink https://www.oecd.org/en/publications/financing-smes-and-entrepreneurs-2020_061fe03d-en/full-report/component-51.html

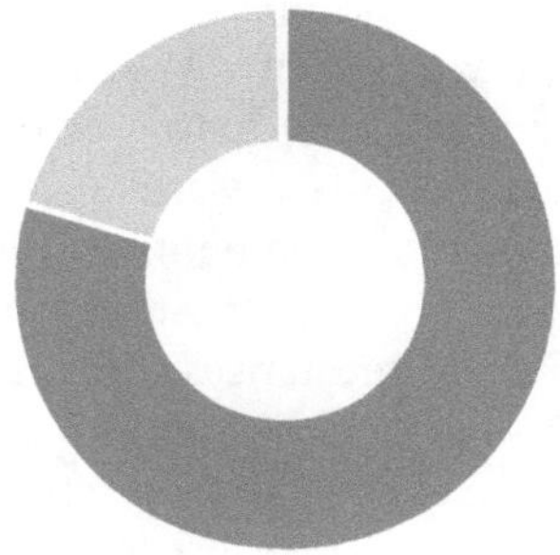

Fig. 5 Outstanding business loans, total accounts for the majority of '2020'. Source: Financing SMEs and Entrepreneurs 2020. An OECD Scoreboard—Statlink https://www.oecd.org/en/publications/financing-smes-and-entrepreneurs-2020_061fe03d-en/full-report/component-51.html

in utilising loans, particularly during pandemics, to remain operational. Minor improvements were observed from 2010 to 2020, especially during the COVID-19 pandemic. This indicates that some businesses viewed loans as an opportunity to sustain themselves, suggesting that other factors warrant further investigation. Regarding additional factors, a relationship exists between levels of education and business success. However, denying entrepreneurs grants based on their educational background could perpetuate inequality. The moral question arises as to whether SMEs with robust business proposals, as evidenced by their levels of education, should receive more support in terms of funding. The intent is to enable those with greater knowledge to assist the government in nurturing a crucial sector that requires development and can yield noticeable results. While education holds significance, the age of SMEs also merits consideration.

3 Risks and Grant Allocation

As literature has already identified, business growth may also result from individual decisions. For instance, the decision to pursue education or obtain technical training extends beyond what policy can effectively address, including managing business risks for success. Furthermore, a risk is associated with allocating grants to businesses and business owners without a guarantee of contributing to the economy or fulfilling the grants'intended purpose. This risks financial loss, which has broader implications for society and the economy. When allocated funds generate employment, some individuals anticipate securing jobs. When South Africa directs its resources explicitly towards exports, it anticipates corresponding benefits in terms of competitive advantage. These factors represent risks when grants are misallocated and their usage cannot be accounted for. Under such circumstances, risks need to be identified and evaluated within policy frameworks. For example, suppose many business owners received funds but did not use them effectively. What is the level of risk to the sustainability of the local economy and to South African society, which has long been plagued by crime and deep inequality even after 1994? Therefore, South Africa may need to contemplate strategies for managing these risks to mitigate the potential decline in national income, especially as the value of productivity appears to be continuously decreasing and is projected to decline further in 2025, putting macroeconomic growth at even greater risk. The Government of National Unity (GNU) offers hope and suggests that corruption may diminish, influencing how the distribution of economic benefits is managed and how associated risks might be mitigated.

One of the ways to reduce risk in managing grants for the government is to examine whether focusing on the needs of a particular country can assist in making decisions regarding grant allocation. This approach involves removing bias associated with the country's history and conducting a needs analysis to establish criteria for grant applications. If the effectiveness of grants allocated to SMEs cannot be determined, the government can explore options that are best suited to the current economic situation and the sustainability of the country in terms of development. One could argue for necessary intervention if the identified risks continue to impact business growth and development. Existing policies in South Africa may need to be reviewed and amended in the context of this argument. The low impact of grants used by SMEs has significant implications, with one major issue being inequality and the need for a new approach to address it. One way to mitigate further risk is to calculate it and assess its size to ascertain the required resources. Therefore, if the risk level decreases, there is a possibility that the effectiveness of policy implementation will improve, along with strategies for allocating grants.

One of South Africa's core values is its Ubuntu philosophy, which emphasises humanity's importance. One would assume that the grant application process could incorporate this ideology and cultural value. The idea is to grant business owners insights into Africanism and humanity while building their brands. It implies that every individual, regardless of social and economic status, can coexist, and one way to ensure this is by using funding to promote essential African values to achieve peace in the community where businesses operate. Therefore, it is necessary first to arrange a business forum to educate business owners and aspiring entrepreneurs on the effective use of funds and how owning a business or having access to funds can foster social cohesion. Similarly, the forum can facilitate crucial collaboration among businesses, allowing them to learn from each other, especially from successful business owners. Literature reveals that successful business owners often hesitate to share what works for them. As a result, new business owners risk failing due to a lack of experience and the absence of mentors who could guide their growth. The government can facilitate mandatory collaboration through policy to mitigate the risk of business failure. This way, the policy and the government will promote humanity in business.

Support in managing and operating businesses in South Africa is crucial to ensuring effective fund utilisation. Support must be comprehensive and holistic to be effective. A key area of support should focus on collaboration, encouraging small businesses to join business associations for knowledge-sharing. However, such relationships should be reciprocal. For instance, individual business owners must identify their needs and the reasons for collaborating with other businesses engaged in similar activities or offering comparable products. The challenge lies in competition. However, we should highlight the potential benefits of collaboration. Negotiation during the collaboration stage is crucial to prevent conflict or financial loss in the partnership. Ultimately, both collaborators should achieve a mutually beneficial agreement.

The essence of allowing change in business management for success is fundamental to an effective business model, particularly for small business owners. While there are likely to be a few competitors who respond to disruptors by exiting the industry, which in turn creates ample opportunities for others, small business owners may need to consider the impact of entering markets that can outspend them in terms of budget and resources. Research suggests that unsuccessful businesses frequently overestimate their ability to form partnerships and invest in significant projects for which they lack the necessary resources. Typically, loans and limited government funding finance these projects. Some companies are bankrupt and must sell assets to pay debts. Premature assumptions of revenue and a lack of skills in determining cash flow have led to failed investment plans for many small businesses.

Therefore, calculating and understanding the value of a business is another crucial aspect for business owners when making investment decisions and acquiring other businesses for growth. This involves evaluating investments or projects to determine the anticipated impact on the sustainability of the business. Therefore, businesses must distinguish between projected cash inflows and outflows that could impact them. While collaboration and venturing into investment projects are encouraged for business growth, these actions also carry risks, and the level of risk must be assessed to avoid losses and potential closure of the business. Therefore, when a business achieves excess funding or exhibits growth, it is advisable to seek the services of a business consultant to maximise the surplus. Part of the decision involves considering how the use of extra funds or surplus, if invested in a project, will affect business owners' wealth, particularly in the long term. A favourable decision is thus desirable, as it indicates that the business will generate a profit from the investment, which means the decision should favour yielding a return. According to the literature, many small businesses in South Africa do not take advantage of opportunities offered by government agencies that can provide support. This support includes, but is not limited to, information and assistance regarding the sustainability of business growth. It is essential to move beyond reliance on government support to ensure the sustainability of their business. However, there is a risk that SMEs may not use funds effectively to generate profits for sustainability, as evidenced by outstanding business loans, primarily from 2020. The rate of return remains low, and debts continue accumulating based on the analysis.

The return earned on the funds by businesses should be aimed at generating additional funds. However, the rate of return will subsequently be compared against competitors to understand how businesses in a segmented market manage the cost of capital and the associated risks. Literature has indicated that the investment of small businesses requires appraisal, particularly for those attempting to venture into franchising and acquisition. Yet, no evidence suggests that these businesses seek financial or business advice before investing. In this context, franchise businesses will adopt a new brand while operating independently. This business decision necessitates oversight by a reliable business consultant. It implies that the business will operate with consideration for other business values and models. The business can likely expect a positive return, but it cannot guarantee the opposite. The loans made and not repaid by SMEs during COVID-19 have consequences for business operations and their ability to secure loans from banks. While arguments can be made regarding the challenges faced during the pandemic, loan repayment indicates that SMEs can manage risks and demonstrate their capacity to generate returns.

One major challenge to pay attention to and determine is the cash flow from venturing into a new business or space. This is often difficult to predict. However, the literature indicates that the increased local competition for small business owners attempting to enter a new space can significantly impact their cash flow and pose a high risk if it is not monitored effectively. The uncertainty surrounding these cash flows could considerably affect the evaluation and analysis of the business. It is essential not to overestimate cash inflows when entering a new business location or in the case of a significant investment. Nevertheless, there is the temptation to anticipate a substantial cash inflow due to the demand generated by new projects and markets. Conversely, by underestimating expected inflows, a business might choose not to pursue what could have been a highly profitable venture. A key issue here is that small businesses are encouraged to employ scenario planning techniques, such as sensitivity analysis or simulation, to explore a range of possible outcomes driven by critical project variables as they plan for growth. These alternative scenarios will allow businesses to understand the impact of investment uncertainty better and highlight the necessity to scrutinise the use of surpluses more closely when making significant investment decisions.

4 Value Analysis

Small businesses in South Africa are in an ecosystem that allows for a value proposition based on excellence due to the opportunities provided by the government. The first step should be to improve the perception of corporate values to attract further opportunities from the business ecosystem. Literature has shown that businesses with strong corporate values attract more funding and investment. Therefore, business owners must identify and analyse opportunities in their environments and allow their corporate values to resonate with them. For instance, businesses that offer excellent customer service and products will likely improve their revenue and create significant value. This includes branding, brand identity, and brand management for their products and services within their business ecosystem; these elements must be established before bringing in employees. There is evidence to support that such businesses break into new markets successfully, making it often difficult for competitors without strong corporate values to displace them. Businesses operate within a highly regulated ecosystem in South Africa. Therefore, businesses should demonstrate value creation and improvement by complying with various government agencies. Customers tend to value and respect businesses with the required licences and the government's permission to operate. Many small businesses in South Africa still struggle to understand the types of permits needed to manage their specific businesses.

Since businesses in South Africa must comply with various regulations to operate, a lack of compliance can cause reputational damage, particularly for businesses that have already established a significant customer base in the market. Consequently, compliance serves as a demonstration of the value system. Government departments are expected to advise businesses to prioritise value by adhering to government regulations and maximising revenue through exceptional customer care. Literature indicates that poor customer service implies a deficient value system and contributes to low revenue generation for most businesses in South Africa. Consequently, businesses should foster their staff's commitment to delivering excellent customer service and enhancing value perception. Given the decline in government funding for SMEs over the years and the market disruption caused by new technology, small business owners must regularly evaluate their business decisions.

In making business decisions, managing costs internally is also important. A cost driver is a factor that causes a change in the cost of an activity for SMEs, which determines their success. Deciding to control costs will mean examining the activities that drive expenses differently within the business. This requires the ability to make strategic decisions about where to focus on business activities without ceasing to create value. Business transformation for success starts with identifying and optimising cost drivers when business owners decide to embark on large projects or invest in new businesses. Cost control aims to maintain profit during investment. Delivering the services business owners require significantly impacts profit, yet these costs remain uncontrolled. Therefore, cost control in this context will also determine the impact of business decisions on profit. This analysis is possible when business owners understand the cost-reduction drivers, such as eliminating non-essential activities that increase expenses. The performance analysis in Fig. 7 shows an increase in outstanding business loans. Although there has been a decline in the number of businesses folding, this number started to rise again during the pandemic. The figure's performance analysis clearly illustrates the inability to manage a business for success.

However, many businesses in South Africa will inevitably face several business risks when collaborating with another company. These risks can be categorised as upsides and downsides. Upside risks refer to those that may allow business owners to seek higher returns and expand their businesses. Risks by nature encompass both upside and downside risks, the latter of which could harm a business' brand. Literature indicates that few small businesses have a strong market reputation due to their inability to create value and manage operational expenses effectively. Identifying and evaluating these business risks is essential to ensure the potential rewards outweigh the associated downside risks.

Studies indicate that companies' most significant business risks include product and reputation risks. During collaborative arrangements, businesses place considerable trust in their partners. The long-term success of such collaborations hinges on the partner's value proposition. The risk

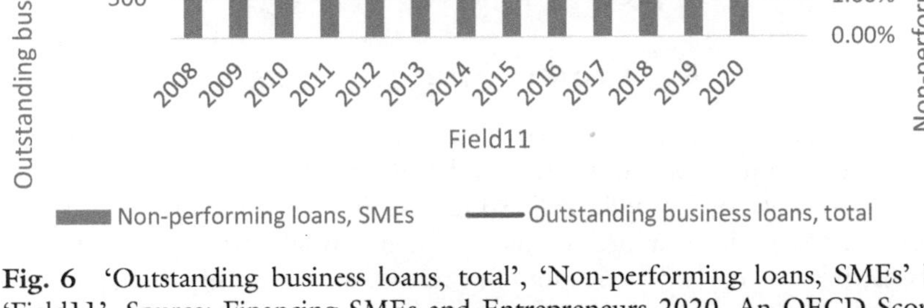

Fig. 6 'Outstanding business loans, total', 'Non-performing loans, SMEs' by 'Field11'. Source: Financing SMEs and Entrepreneurs 2020. An OECD Scoreboard—Statlink https://www.oecd.org/en/publications/financing-smes-and-entrepreneurs-2020_061fe03d-en/full-report/component-51.html

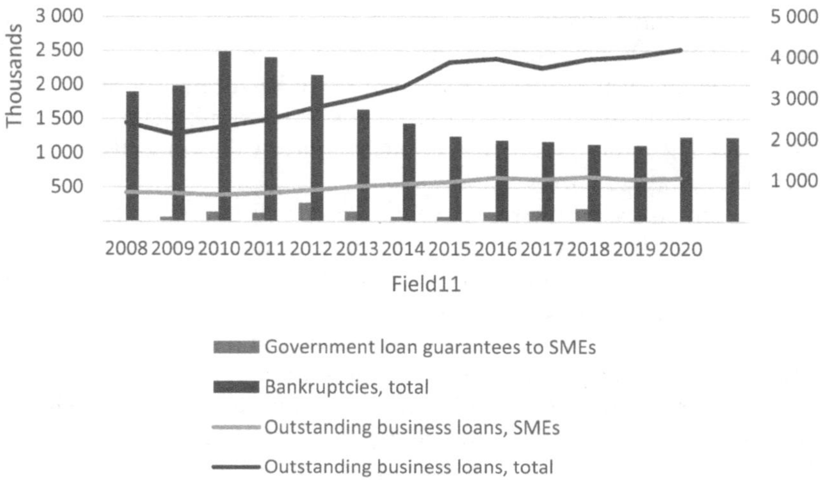

Fig. 7 Performance Analysis. Source: Financing SMEs and Entrepreneurs 2020. An OECD Scoreboard—Statlink https://www.oecd.org/en/publications/financing-smes-and-entrepreneurs-2020_061fe03d-en/full-report/component-51.html

escalates if the partner organisation exerts control over other businesses. Consequently, SMEs should ensure that their contractual agreements adequately protect them from potential product and reputation risks by clearly stipulating their expectations from a joint partner. This approach will likely result in establishing a service level agreement with a partner that explicitly defines the minimum standards and quality requirements that the partner must deliver as part of the contractual arrangement.

5 Concluding Remarks

The analysis indicates that the South African government has continued to finance small businesses and business development, but has not addressed the weaknesses of its policy. The increase in debts incurred by SMEs indicates the policy's failure to analyse the potential performance of businesses that could yield corresponding results for economic development. Similarly, the number of closed businesses serves as further evidence that the policy is ineffective. The prevalence of informal businesses adds to the challenges of measuring the adequate performance of loans, funds, and the contribution of small businesses in the country. Despite this, the Department of Small Business has proposed criteria to support businesses affected by COVID-19, offering a preferential interest rate of 5%. These businesses must be duly registered with CIPC, SARS, and UIF. This policy evaluates the challenges surrounding using loans and other funds disbursed to SMEs, particularly during pandemics. The SARB/NT has provided approximately ZAR 200 billion in guaranteed loans to SMEs through South African commercial banks. Additionally, through the Township and Rural Entrepreneurship Programme, the government has allocated around ZAR 740 million in loans and grants to informal businesses. Therefore, while it has programmes and policies to support SMEs that are comprehensive, they lack a performance-based approach, which explains the low contributions of SMEs to economic development.

The policy and intention for SMEs' development are clear. What is unclear is the effectiveness of these policies at the recipient level. For example, if township residents are trained in business and how to access opportunities, how long will it take for them to use funding to meet policy goals? Corresponding results are anticipated from individuals who are predominantly unprepared for business development. The policies conceived since 1994 appear to inadequately address the factors contributing to the success of business enterprises. An excessive focus on funding may pose a challenge if the remnants of past damages are not rectified. However, 30 years of democracy should have brought about considerable improvements. The current unemployment rate reflects the policy failures in business development in South Africa. This issue further exacerbates inequalities and disparities in funding distribution and assessment. This represents yet another form of inequality in the post-apartheid era, driven by how policies are conceptualised.

Meanwhile, there is a profound emphasis on ensuring accountability in relation to performance of small business. This translates into how to monitor and evaluate SMEs' performance. There are several ways to monitor and evaluate how government intervention for business has performed over the year. Literature and data have established problems of accountability and performance over the years. Therefore, Theory of Change or its ideas can be used to determine what strategies are appropriate to design and implement a small business operation in South Africa. Among other things, a theory of change will allow the government to review its inputs in terms of funds, process, and/or impacts. In the context of SMEs in South Africa, resources are grants and other supports, including training afforded to small business owners or beneficiaries. These interventions connect to performance. The only possible way to measure the performance of a business is when it uses the resources to generate profits, and if these profits are sufficient, they can lead to job creation. This framework, if applied holistically, can redefine ways to measure accountability or assess the performance of SME support. In other words, South Africa needs to review indicators used to measure the performance of SME support to include impact on society and economy. Based on this framework, South Africa's inputs, such as funds and training for SMEs, will be clearly defined for impact purposes. Because the government wants to ensure the failure of businesses at an early stage, there is a need to devote more resources to business development training, particularly for beneficiaries from rural communities. The expectation is that outputs in terms of SMEs supported will increase, but in proportion to innovative solution businesses. This theory in application means if the government equips business owners with innovative digital solutions, for instance, the outcomes will be increased job creation and reduced unemployment in the country, both in the short and long run. This is the only way the government could measure the impact of SME support. SMEs' support is impactful if transformation extends to sustainable economic development, reduction in poverty, crime, and unemployment. Studies have shown that performance measurements that are focused beyond the number of beneficiaries but embrace indicators such as socio-economic impact are reliable. Likewise, evidence-based decision-making will lead to sustainable change. In the context of South Africa, accountability and transparency in the use of funds and the process of providing intervention will be part of the elements to ensure impactful change.

References

Abe, M., Troilo, M., & Batsaikhan, O. (2015). Financing small and medium enterprises in Asia and the Pacific. *Journal of Entrepreneurship and Public Policy, 4*(1), 2–32.

Abisuga-Oyekunle, O. A., Patra, S. K., & Muchie, M. (2020). SMEs in sustainable development: Their role in poverty reduction and employment generation in sub-Saharan Africa. *African Journal of Science, Technology, Innovation and Development, 12*(4), 405–419.

Adebisi, S. A., Alaneme, G. C., & Ofuani, A. B. (2015). Challenges of finance and the performance of small and medium enterprises (SMES) in Lagos State.

Baporikar, N., Nambira, G., & Gomxos, G. (2016). Exploring factors hindering SMEs growth: Evidence from Nambia. *Journal of Science and Technology Policy Management, 7*(2), 190–211.

Bushe, B. (2019). The causes and impact of business failure among small to micro and medium enterprises in South Africa. *Africa's Public Service Delivery and Performance Review, 7*(1), 1–26.

Enwereji, C. P., Aluko, T. O., & Bayai, I. (2023). South African government palliative funds for SMMEs during COVID-19: Challenges of implementation and suggestions for improvement.

Fielden, S. L., Davidson, M. J., & Makin, P. J. (2000). Barriers encountered during micro and small business start-up in north-West England. *Journal of Small Business and Enterprise Development, 7*(4), 295–304.

Joseph, T., Obikaonu, P., Ariolu, C., Nwolisa, C., & Aderohunmu, A. (2021). Smes intervention programmes in Nigeria: Evaluating challenges facing implementation. *Applied Journal of Economics, Management and Social Sciences, 2*(1), 16–25.

Leboea, S. T. (2017). The factors influencing SME failure in South Africa.

Maduekwe, C. C., & Kamala, P. (2016). Performance measurement by small and medium enterprises in Cape Metropolis, South Africa. *Problems and Perspectives in Management, 14*(2), 46–55.

Megersa, K. (2020). Improving SMEs access to finance through capital markets and innovative financing instruments: Some evidence from developing countries.

Msomi, T. S., & Olarewaju, O. M. (2021). Factors affecting small and medium enterprises financial sustainability in South Africa. *African Journal of Inter/Multidisciplinary Studies, 3*(1), 103–117.

Njue, N. G. (2021). *Implementation of Jua-kalis-empowerment Programme, Risk Management Practice and Performance of Micro-small-entrepreneurial Projects in Nairobi County, Kenya* (Doctoral dissertation, University of Nairobi).

Opute, A. P., Chukwuma-Nwuba, O., Iwu, C. G., Eniola, A. A., Ojra, J., & Irene, J. (2022). Productive entrepreneurship: Entrepreneurial networking perspective and research agenda. In *The Future of Entrepreneurship in Africa* (pp. 222–234).

Park, S., & Liang, J. (2020). Merit, diversity, and performance: Does diversity management moderate the effect of merit principles on governmental performance? *Public Personnel Management, 49*(1), 83–110.

Peter, F., Adegbuyi, O., Olokundun, M., Peter, A. O., Amaihian, A. B., & Ibidunni, A. S. (2018). Government financial support and financial performance of SMEs. *Academy of Strategic Management Journal, 17*.

Prasannath, V., Adhikari, R. P., Gronum, S., & Miles, M. P. (2024). Impact of government support policies on entrepreneurial orientation and SME performance. *International Entrepreneurship and Management Journal, 20*(3), 1533–1595.

Smith, H., Discetti, R., Bellucci, M., & Acuti, D. (2022). SMEs engagement with the sustainable development goals: A power perspective. *Journal of Business Research, 149*, 112–122.

Solani, M. (2020). *The use and effectiveness of financial performance measures in small and medium enterprises (SMEs) retail businesses in Cape Town* (Doctoral dissertation, Cape Peninsula University of Technology).

Thompson Agyapong, G., Mmieh, F., & Mordi, C. (2018). Factors influencing the growth of SMEs: The case of Ghana. *Thunderbird International Business Review, 60*(4), 549–563.

Van Niekerk, A. P. (2019). *The perception of broad-based Black economic empowerment (BBBEE) in small and medium enterprises* (Doctoral dissertation, North-West University).

CHAPTER 5

Public Investment Subsidy and Challenges of Accountability in South Africa

1 Introduction

According to OECD (2022), there are approximately 2.6 million small, micro, and medium enterprises (SMMEs), with around 37% classified as formal businesses. Among these, 54% are micro-enterprises, and 15% operate in rural areas. The owners of these businesses are individuals who have seized identified opportunities, as well as those who have started their enterprises out of necessity due to a lack of alternative income sources. Two-thirds of small and medium-sized enterprise (SME) proprietors operate their enterprises without employing any personnel, while thirty-two per cent have between one and ten employees. Despite the fact that their growth rate over the past decade has been lagging behind general economic growth, the contribution of SMMEs to South Africa's gross value added (akin to GDP before taxes and subsidies) increased significantly from 18% in 2010 to 40% in 2020. Only 34% of these organisations maintain official financial accounts under their respective identities. The convergence of consumer and commercial credit often results in several challenges, including the adoption of inappropriate financial products, increased risk of personal debt accumulation, diminished borrowing capacity for owners, negative impacts on owners' credit profiles, and violations of company law and accounting standards. The demand for financing among SMMEs is largely influenced by entrepreneurs' aspirations and market opportunities, which are, to some

T. O. Aluko, *Evaluation of Small Business Support in Post-Apartheid South Africa*, https://doi.org/10.1007/978-981-95-2864-6_5

extent, affected by the broader macroeconomic environment. As of the end of 2020, banks extended a total credit of ZAR 631 billion to SMMEs, representing 25% of all business loans, according to the South African Reserve Bank (SARB).

However, significant improvements in funding for these enterprises appear improbable without addressing additional critical factors necessary for their growth and sustainability, including market access, business acumen, management skills, and financial literacy. Increased developmental support is essential, particularly to promote the formalisation of SMEs. From 2010 to 2020, the non-performing loan rate in the SME sector declined from 5.2% to 4.9%. This figure increased from 3.1% in 2019, influenced by the global COVID-19 pandemic. The government offers financial support to SMEs through grants, direct loans, and guarantees facilitated by development finance institutions (DFIs). Furthermore, credit guarantees are employed in South Africa, and the government is contemplating the establishment of a movable collateral registry and credit information database to reduce lending risks, potentially enhancing access to bank financing. A revised partial credit guarantee scheme will enhance these initiatives. Accountability, both as a concept and in practical application, must be understood within the context of the complexities and dynamics of funding, particularly regarding the policy framework that has supported SMEs in South Africa since 1994. The distribution of Black-owned SMEs by informal and formal sectors is highlighted in the Global Entrepreneurship Monitor (GEM) South Africa report (2023). The data shows informal business accounts for about 70% and the process to formalise these businesses has been slow. Herrington & Kew (2016) and Fatoki (2012) have mentioned in their findings that the lack of skills and the problem of capacity building, including lack of access to finance and regulation issues, have made formalisation of business a challenge. This also includes trust issues in the government and the cost of complying with requirements to formalise the business (Rogerson, 2018).

2 SMEs and Accountability

The post-apartheid economic transformation concept enables an analysis of the financing structure for businesses in South Africa. There exists a significant assumption that financing could foster broader economic development. This assumption, however, overlooks issues of accountability. The global context of financing for entrepreneurs presents diverse dynamics, predominantly facilitated through government interventions or programmes. Nevertheless, implementing various government programmes for business owners has faced challenges in accountability, not only in developing countries. Studies have examined the implementation of the Small Business Act in Europe to gain insights into the business environment for SMEs (The European Commission, 2014). The focus of this study is instrumental in elucidating the reasons behind the improvements in the growth of business enterprises in developed countries. In essence, there has been an effort to support business owners through research to understand systemic challenges further. While the systemic issues in Europe differ according to economic and political contexts, there is a prevailing trend among European governments to enhance their support for small businesses. The historical context of South Africa is intricately linked to the allocation of finances for small businesses, as characterised by the necessity for macroeconomic development after 1994. Consequently, economic transformation interventions have resulted in a significant increase of 91% in business establishments post-1994, compared to only 8.7% during apartheid, which indicates effective policy (Kongolo, 2010). This suggests that the number of Black individuals with business registrations rose markedly in the post-apartheid era, and they have benefited from policies that fund their initiatives and promote their growth. The objective of transformation policies for small business development after 1994 was to empower South Africans, particularly Black individuals who were victims of economic deprivation due to resource scarcity. Nevertheless, resources come in various forms, and financial resources were not the primary reason for policy failures in establishing an economy before liberation (Bushe, 2019).

One of the notable characteristics of the late twentieth and early twenty-first centuries is the redefinition of the role and significance of global economies. This has become increasingly important due to the growing necessity for small business owners to integrate into the global community. There is an assumption that small businesses, which are accountable for using funds, can readily expand beyond the confines of their local environments. In this context, globalisation has prompted evolving perspectives on the importance of localities within an increasingly interconnected global framework, highlighting the influence of economic norms, independent initiatives, and the pursuit of innovative strategies to navigate this transformative economic landscape. This is particularly relevant for SMEs seeking additional funding for expansion, where accountability is multidimensional. One aspect pertains to the efficient use of every fund, while another involves devising strategies to secure their brands' acceptance both locally and globally. In other words, accountability embodies the mindset of progressive SMEs. Therefore, progressive SMEs judiciously leverage government grants to foster trust, thereby promoting growth and expansion. After 30 years of democracy, society is demanding accountability from the government and extending to the policies that fund SMEs.

Following the transition to democracy in 1994, the development of the small, medium, and micro-enterprise (SMME) sector has emerged as a primary emphasis of governmental policy in South Africa. The presence of high unemployment and poverty rates in urban areas underscores the importance of this policy for urban development. The national government seeks to enhance opportunities for businesses owned by Black South Africans, acknowledging the complex historical context and the disadvantages faced during apartheid. A study indicates that existing policy frameworks recognise the national government's constrained capacity to independently improve the competitiveness of Black-owned SMMEs, leading to heightened support for private-sector initiatives. The government encounters difficulties in implementing its principles, particularly in utilising its procurement power to benefit Black-owned SMMEs (Rogerson, 2013). The capacity to finance SMEs has recently improved due to advocacy for substantial small business development, contributing to national economic growth and enhancing global competitiveness. Concerns exist regarding the potential oversight of accountability within these funding systems in the policy. This involves evaluating the attributes of businesses and their owners in addition to the social inclusion agenda. Assessors may be overlooked, and the policy may lack clarity regarding the measurement of accountability and the specific obligations of grant holders.

Accountability is a concept that illustrates the prudent use of government funds. In the context of governmental support for small businesses, both those responsible for fund allocation and distribution and the entrepreneurs who may have received grants must demonstrate the responsible use of taxpayers' money for societal development. Research has highlighted the importance of small and medium enterprises (SMEs) in fostering local economic growth in South Africa. This growth occurs when SMEs use the funds to generate profits and contribute positively to their communities. Accountability suggests that SMEs have surmounted significant challenges in achieving results. However, numerous businesses in rural areas struggle to yield outcomes and adequately account for the funds they receive. A study indicates that a significant challenge local governments in Limpopo Province face is the lack of sufficient human and financial resources to deliver essential services and maintain critical infrastructure (Nkwinika & Munzhedzi, 2016). The inability of local governments to provide basic social amenities could potentially hinder businesses that strive to contribute to their communities, which implies that a lack of accountability from the government can also adversely affect government programmes, as these will only thrive in an environment that nurtures and encourages entrepreneurial activities. Hence, despite government fund allocation to support to SMEs, there is no assurance of effective utilisation of those funds if the business environment remains volatile, insecure, and problematic. Accountability, therefore, operates in two directions: in the context of both funders and fund users.

3 Power Dynamic of Public Funds

According to Section 229 of the 1996 South African Constitution, municipalities in South Africa have extensive revenue-generating powers. These powers include user fees, property rates, and surcharges on municipally delivered or rendered services. Sections 224 and 227 also ensure that municipalities receive an appropriate part of the national revenue collected, considering their distinctive roles, fiscal capacities, and developmental requirements. This statute states that local governments may use public funds for development objectives. As a result, being accountable to the community is essential for development. Thus, SMEs are local governments' partners who can help them achieve growth. This cooperation is based on the notion that SMEs can make significant contributions to the community, as well as the government's commitment to provide them with the necessary support. For example, electricity and potable water availability is critical for producing and distributing basic goods in local markets. A shortage of these resources might impede productivity and cause issues for SMEs. Businesspeople receive ongoing support after receiving funds. The government will generally fulfil its constitutional commitment to transparency in its financial reporting and development assistance.

However, Section 227(2) releases the national government from the obligation to compensate municipalities that fail to generate revenue following their fiscal capacities and tax bases. Additionally, it shields municipalities that show fiscal effort from penalties. Therefore, relying solely on government transfers may not effectively address all the service delivery challenges and backlogs that municipalities face. According to the National Treasury (2011, p. 205), these transfers are intended to supplement local revenues, focusing on improving services for low-income households and addressing infrastructure shortages in rural areas. If local governments should generate more revenue to sustain their communities, there is a need for an honest approach to create a vibrant entrepreneurial culture. This means a deliberate attempt to transform the local economy using purposive collaboration with SMEs. There is a possibility of generating more revenue and ensuring stability if such collaboration is well defined and followed up without corruption. However, such a partnership requires caution, particularly in how taxes are administered for SMEs.

A study has examined the tax functions of small and medium-sized manufacturing businesses in Gauteng Province, South Africa. Based on the study's findings, this research highlights the key challenges these SMEs face when managing government taxes. It primarily focuses on the administration process rather than the taxes themselves. The study has observed that tax compliance requirements in South Africa pose a significant barrier for SMEs. They recommend that the government consider reducing the number of taxes that SMEs must manage, lowering compliance obligations, and providing additional resources to assist these businesses in handling their tax administration (Abrie & Doussy, 2006). While taxes generate funds and are part of accounting for SMEs, there is a pressing need to further support small businesses, particularly those in rural communities, by simplifying tax processes and offering incentives to ensure they are not discouraged from continuing operations. However, the government must fulfil its obligations to ensure that those required to pay taxes do so, especially businesses that have developed over time. It is crucial to resolve the complications often accompanying tax preparation and compliance for SMEs, particularly for individuals with little or no education. While accountability is vital in these areas, context should also inform business policy in the country, including tax policies. Governments must demonstrate accountability by showing how their policies specifically support Black women-owned businesses. Additionally, there is a need to illustrate the contributions of business owners to the development of local communities and nations. Such evidence is essential to demonstrate genuine transformation; therefore, allocation and support for Black business owners must reflect such commitment.

However, research has identified that financial support significantly influences the performance of SMEs. Still, this assistance is often inadequate and characterised by rigid, unrealistic bureaucratic requirements, which may contribute to non-accountability issues. Based on this finding, the study suggested that improving access to adequate funding could greatly enhance the performance of SMEs (Kato, 2024). On the other hand, an increase in funding does not necessarily equate to increased productivity. Providing more funding to businesses and owners without accountability for previous funds indicates policy failure. While a lack of access to funds can restrict the capacity of SMEs willing to support the government's agenda for transformation, there is a pressing need for policy review to prevent wastage. Establishing bureaucratic requirements often creates opportunities for corruption, a problem prevalent in many developing countries. However, this situation must be addressed, as a lack of transparency will continue to foster irresponsibility, non-accountability, and struggles for essential development factors such as SMEs. Thus, there exists a power dynamic within the policy framework. The interaction between a national government that formulates policy, the individuals responsible for implementation, and businesspeople entrusted with grants is complex. The expectation is that the government can leverage its authority to review policies to improve access to support or funding while simultaneously dismantling the power structures that exploit the system or impede accountability among the involved parties.

4 Financing Accountable SMEs

The cost of borrowing is a significant factor for businesses that may find bank financing viable. The cost of borrowing, coupled with the inability to grow following government support for businesses, has been identified in the literature as a reason for the failure of many establishments after 1994. In most instances, the majority of small enterprises opt for non-credit options to finance their operations (Kongolo, 2010). Business sustainability cannot rely solely on government programmes and funding for long-term survival. It is essential for business owners to be aware of alternative means for growth, as the economy requires more large businesses to generate higher revenue, employment, and development simultaneously. Even if policies enabled financial resources to be accessible in the pre-apartheid era, there was no evidence to suggest that Black-owned businesses would thrive (Ssekitoleko & du Plessis, 2021).

However, small businesses in townships are distinct. They differ due to their informality and require less financial investment and policy oversight. Despite this, these communities often have limited access to funding and information regarding sustainability. Rural communities need the capacity to develop themselves, including ensuring that policies foster an environment where small business activities can flourish through support mechanisms beyond mere funding. Since 1994, crime levels have remained high, and rural development has been slow in many townships (Clack & Minnaar, 2018). One of the funding policy objectives for small businesses is to reduce crime by creating jobs, which should ultimately lead to development. In other words, while significant funding has been allocated to townships, it is often not used effectively or made accessible to them (Shackleton et al., 2018). This issue is not one of policy but rather of human factors. The argument is that financial support for small businesses in townships may not lead to transformation or accountability unless the human aspect of the funding is more thoroughly examined.

The South African government has funded small businesses since 1994, but has been blamed for focusing resources on well-resourced industries and ignoring important sectors for economic growth (Irene, 2017). Many argue that funded and developed businesses and industries do not contribute to South Africa's broader economic development. Recently, digital transformation has also disrupted small businesses, hindering township businesses or business owners' ability to succeed. The government is expected to look more closely at changes in the global business market and the effect of technology as a strategic intervention to grow essential sectors. In Malaysia, the issue of financing gaps in small and medium enterprises (SMEs) is common. Financing gaps arise when SMEs do not have the necessary funds to operate or expand their businesses. This financing gap arises from a disparity between the demand for and the supply of institutional funding for SMEs. In South Africa, the government has identified a segment of the population requiring urgent business support. As such, the focus on the needy has framed business development since 1994. Although SMEs often claim that funding is readily available, they struggle to access bank financing. Unlike government grants, banks will ensure strict compliance and conduct thorough background checks on applicants for affordability and accountability purposes. On the other hand, banks contend that their limited lending to SMEs is due to a lack of qualified demand. This situation highlights the persistent financing gap faced by many developing countries, including South Africa. This research aims to deepen our understanding of the financing gap, traditionally analysed primarily from a demand perspective (Ramlee & Berma, 2013).

Over the past 15 years, South Africa has increasingly committed to developing business incubation as part of broader initiatives to strengthen the small enterprise sector. The essence of business incubation is to provide additional support to SMEs that require, for instance, training and other enhancements in business management for accountability purposes. There is a possibility that business incubators will expand and be successful in utilising grants, with accountability being an integral part of the business incubation process. The research conducted by Masutha and Rogerson (2015) explores the various pathways of modern business incubation in South Africa, focusing on both the different trajectories and the common challenges encountered by the emerging network of state-supported and private-sector incubators. In this context, entrepreneurial competencies are vital for achieving business success. The study differentiates between the trait and competency approaches when analysing the factors contributing to business success.

Notably, female entrepreneurs in South Africa perceive and value the competency variable differently. Similarly, there are cultural differences in the application of entrepreneurial competencies among the four main racial groups in the country. Research has comprehensively analysed the competency variable in relation to the factors influencing business success for female entrepreneurs in South Africa. It establishes a foundation for a focused agenda on training and developing entrepreneurial competencies among South African female entrepreneurs (Irene, 2017). The evidence suggests that the accountability of grants by SMEs varies by race and gender in South Africa. Therefore, it is important for policymakers to use this information to improve grant systems for SMEs.

4.1 Challenges

The three primary challenges identified for small, micro, and medium-sized enterprises (SMMEs) in the Vaal Triangle region of Gauteng Province are difficulties in obtaining loans, a shortage of training opportunities, and a lack of entrepreneurial skills, ranked in order of significance.

Consequently, these challenges are likely to lead to reduced accountability. The study also found that securing loans on favourable terms from microlenders is a significant barrier for SMMEs in this region. There is insufficient information regarding the reasons for the inability to access loans. For bank loans, a lack of accountability for the use of previous grants and the ability to manage a business successfully are often considered the measures of accountability by many financial institutions. To address these challenges, it has been recommended that the Department of Trade and Industry support SMMEs by establishing comprehensive mentorship, monitoring, and evaluation programmes (Ndege & Park, 2015). A review of the literature reveals that SMMEs in the Vaal Triangle experience a high failure rate. So, how can the government address these challenges through mentorship to ensure that businesspeople in this region take responsibility for the use of public funds? Mentorship models may include the responsibility of SMEs to the government, society, and localities in which their businesses are located. In other words, mentorship helps entrepreneurs realise that their lack of success directly impacts their communities' growth.

On the other hand, the importance of credit in promoting entrepreneurial activities is noted in the literature. In the case of Tanzanian government financial institutions, a significant increase in business output was observed after SMEs had access to financing. The findings show that trained business owners who received advisory support performed better than those who did not. Furthermore, the study emphasises that many challenges entrepreneurs face are not primarily related to a lack of capital but stem from macroeconomic and institutional constraints. Challenges include inadequate infrastructure and intense competition among micro and small-scale producers (Kuzilwa, 2005). In this case, the government makes accountability difficult for successful SMEs that are trained to use their business to contribute to economic development.

Additionally, research highlights the challenges faced by small and medium-sized enterprises (SMEs) when applying for bank loans from various financial institutions in Ghana, including both banks and non-bank entities. These loans are crucial for supporting daily business operations and pursuing expansion projects, which, in turn, contribute to poverty alleviation and job creation. Although some financial institutions are willing to lend to SMEs, many Ghanaian SMEs struggle to meet the requisite criteria, particularly the collateral requirement, which is often unattainable. Furthermore, the limited equity base of these small and medium-sized enterprises presents an additional hurdle. SMEs that manage to secure credit frequently encounter high interest rates and short repayment periods, hindering their capacity to invest in growth or development initiatives. Another pressing issue is the high rate of loan repayment defaults, often linked to constrained cash flow situations caused by difficulties in managing accounts receivable. The study concludes with recommendations aimed at enhancing the SME sector's access to capital. These include enforcing the Credit Reporting Act, encouraging financial institutions to provide factoring services, and offering tax incentives to banks that lend to SMEs to foster more favourable lending practices (Ackah & Vuvor, 2011). In the context of Ghana, there appears to be a tendency to support SMEs, despite historical instances of poor performance and accountability in fund usage. This suggests that policy interventions could be implemented to address concerns about accountability and performance. For instance, small and medium-sized enterprises (SMEs) require improved technical assistance, which includes understanding the implications of financial decisions and their related accountability.

For instance, small and medium-sized Enterprises (SMEs) across various regions are currently drawing significant attention, particularly regarding global accounting and reporting. This heightened interest is mainly due to the introduction of International Financial Reporting Standards (IFRS), specifically designed for SMEs. Evidence suggests that adopting these standards can pose challenges for non-publicly accountable entities, revealing several conceptual and practical issues associated with their implementation. The analyses and insights from this research will have implications for revising the IFRS for SMEs and will assist in addressing potential complications in the convergence process (Perera & Chand, 2015). Accountability for SMEs may not necessarily stem from non-compliance but rather from the complexity of various factors affecting their business, particularly accounting-related ones.

Despite various government initiatives, SMEs often struggle to succeed in a competitive market. In the study of SMEs in the Lephalale Local Municipality, SMEs face significant barriers in sustaining their operations, primarily due to limited access to essential equipment and financial resources. Furthermore, many SMEs have expressed an interest in undertaking bookkeeping training. They also face challenges in competing with larger businesses as a result of these resource constraints. This research recommends that SMEs collaborate to enhance their business skills.

Additionally, it suggests that the government should reassess existing standards to better support SMEs in achieving their development goals (Majadibodu, 2023).

4.2 *Financial Institutions*

There is evidence that, on average, state financial institutions worldwide have underperformed, failing to meet even the lowest expectations. Issues such as poor governance, inadequate management skills, lack of regulation and transparency, and misguided incentives have tarnished the reputation of these institutions in their role of supporting the development of local financial markets. However, the active participation of some state financial institutions during recent crises—especially in providing loans to sectors that commercial banks usually avoid—has sparked new discussions about the possible benefits of state ownership in banking. Research has examined four state financial institutions that have historically performed relatively well: Canada's Business Development Bank, Chile's Banco Estado, South Africa's Development Bank of Southern Africa, and Finland's Finnvera plc. The study discovered that these institutions implement diverse mechanisms to prevent potential mismanagement of resources. Additionally, the author notes that advancements in assessing the policy performance of these institutions have been limited (Rudolph, 2009).

In terms of policy performance evaluation, research analyses (Krasniqi, 2010) show data from a 2006 SME survey conducted by the Riinvest Institute to investigate the factors influencing the likelihood of securing bank financing following an application. The survey results indicate that not all firms can obtain the credit they seek, suggesting a slight imbalance where demand for credit exceeds supply. The findings also show that commercial banks primarily base their lending decisions on collateral. Firms that perform well tend to pursue credit due to optimistic future business outlooks; however, profitability alone does not appear to be a sufficient indicator for banks in making credit allocation decisions.

In 2006, the government introduced a strategic plan to attain middle-income status by 2030, identifying small and medium enterprises (SMEs) as essential contributors to this initiative. The Equity Group Foundation (EGF) supported this effort by providing credit facilities and financial literacy resources to SMEs. Representing over 99% of all businesses worldwide, SMEs play a vital role in promoting economic growth in both rural and urban areas, facilitating balanced development.

The overall success of the global economy is closely linked to the performance of SMEs. In response to this need, Equity Bank launched a financial literacy programme to equip SMEs with crucial financial skills. In Kenya, SMEs face challenges such as inadequate training and management capabilities, which undermine their resilience to risks and impede their growth. The issue of loan repayment among SMEs, with specific objectives focusing on the impacts of bookkeeping, credit management, and budgeting, has become prominent as a result (Mutegi et al., 2015).

5 Accountability for Black-Owned Small and Medium Enterprises

In South Africa, there has been a significant rise in Black-owned small and medium enterprises (SMEs), especially within the construction sector. However, many of these businesses continue encountering various challenges that adversely affect their accountability and performance. Research has explored the internal factors impacting the performance of Black-owned SMEs in the South African construction industry and identified five key constraints affecting business performance: occupational health and safety, human resources, leadership style, workplace communication, and resource allocation (Mafundu & Mafini, 2019). A study evaluated whether the Black Economic Empowerment (BEE) Act has created new economic opportunities for historically disadvantaged South Africans or has contributed to an increased impoverishment within lower-class communities. This analysis is based on a thorough review of existing research, which indicates that even though BEE has been around for many years, it has led to the rise of social classes because of issues such as fraud, corruption, fronting, and challenges in checking people's status, political interference, and poor accountability. The study also scrutinises the local government's implementation of BEE to determine its effectiveness in addressing historical inequalities. The study concludes that the government should reassess BEE as an economic empowerment strategy to evaluate its benefits for the Black majority. Furthermore, it emphasises that BEE requires proper implementation and alignment with other economic initiatives, such as the National Development Plan, to enhance economic opportunities for the Black majority. Additionally, it suggests that the South African government, particularly at the local municipality level, should prioritise the monitoring and evaluating BEE procurement systems to prevent manipulation and corruption related to tender awards in local government (Shava, 2016).

5.1 Local Governments

Local government is often regarded as the tier of government closest to the citizens. In most countries, it generally represents the third sphere of governance. South Africa's governmental structure consists of three distinct yet interconnected spheres. The Constitution of the Republic of South Africa, enacted in 1996, delineates the distribution of powers and responsibilities among these spheres, ensuring that one does not infringe upon the jurisdiction of another. The country is organised into three types of municipalities: Category A (metropolitan), Category B (urban), and Category C (district). A notable challenge is that nearly 60% of the population resides in urban areas. Post-apartheid, municipalities were restructured into non-racial entities that included vast rural regions, many of which contain economically disadvantaged communities that struggle to contribute financially toward the services they receive. As a result, municipalities frequently rely on national government grants to provide essential services such as water, electricity, waste removal, and sanitation (Oosthuizen & Thornhill, 2017).

Soga (2022) examines the implementation of e-government as a strategy to enhance services for small, medium, and micro-enterprises (SMMEs) within the South African context, specifically focusing on the City of Johannesburg (CoJ) and the City of Tshwane (CoT) as case studies. The findings revealed that the two local governments examined are not effectively addressing the challenges faced by SMMEs, which include inadequate access to funding, limited market opportunities, skills and capacity deficiencies among entrepreneurs, insufficient infrastructure, low technology access, and excessive regulation. Consequently, the study recommends establishing a framework for e-government and SMMEs that aims to implement or enhance e-government services, thereby optimising government support for SMMEs. This strategy is based on the belief that e-government can address many of the challenges faced by SMMEs in South Africa, given the existence of various support systems currently hindered by poor coordination, inadequate engagement with beneficiaries, unnecessary bureaucracy, and corruption.

Similarly, there is a need to explore the crucial role of small and medium enterprises (SMEs) in the economy. The importance of SMEs can be discussed in how they support existing businesses while encouraging the establishment of new start-ups. The significant contribution of SMEs to Local Economic Development (LED) is widely recognised. In developing countries, SMEs are essential for job creation for several reasons: they foster entrepreneurship; by employing local residents, small businesses help reduce risks, including lowering crime rates; they contribute to building systemic productive capacities and creating resilient economic systems by facilitating connections between small and large enterprises. Additionally, SMEs typically use more labour-intensive production methods than larger firms, enhancing employment opportunities and promoting fairer income distribution. They also create livelihood opportunities through simple, value-added processing activities, particularly in agricultural economics (Ayandibu & Houghton, 2017).

Comparatively, trade and economic liberalisation policies have adversely affected the operations of small to medium enterprises (SMEs) in both Zimbabwe and South Africa. These financially constrained SMEs are struggling to compete against resource-rich multinational corporations. The situation is dire, and without significant government intervention, the future of SMEs appears bleak. Furthermore, most SMEs in both countries are not engaged in exporting due to a lack of knowledge and resources, and their capacity for innovation remains considerably low. The research indicates no significant differences in the impacts of trade liberalisation reforms on SMEs in Zimbabwe compared to those in South Africa. It is recommended that both governments implement incentives to encourage SMEs to export and create more jobs. Additionally, when negotiating the entry conditions for multinationals, Zimbabwe and South Africa should prioritise technology transfer to SMEs. Reintroducing tariffs in critical economic sectors is also suggested to limit the influx of cheap imports. The study cautions that failing to protect SMEs could jeopardise their survival in both Zimbabwe and South Africa, potentially resulting in higher unemployment rates, increased poverty, and growing wealth inequality (Chingwaru, 2014).

Furthermore, a study examines the opportunities and challenges related to local revenue mobilisation in Anglophone Africa, focusing on urban areas. It analyses various revenue mechanisms and their implications for economic efficiency, income distribution, and accountability. The discussion highlights the political and administrative obstacles hindering different revenue instruments and the factors influencing citizen compliance. A key conclusion is that while local revenue collected by most local government authorities in Africa is essential, it is insufficient to develop and provide services for the rapidly growing population adequately. There is a need to improve local government revenue mobilisation in Africa.

It is interesting to note that these problems are not peculiar to Africa alone. Small and medium-sized enterprises (SMEs) are fundamental to the Asian economy, accounting for over 98% of businesses in the region and generating two out of three jobs in the private sector. Consequently, effective support systems for SMEs are essential for the economic prosperity of Asia. However, SMEs face several challenges that impede their growth, including limited access to financing, a lack of comprehensive databases, low research and development (R&D) spending, underdeveloped sales channels, and restricted financial inclusion. A study shows inadequate financing, lack of comprehensive databases, minimal R&D investments, and insufficient use of information technology as major factors contributing to the slow growth of SMEs in Asia (Yoshino & Taghizadeh Hesary, 2016). Africa and Asia have unique challenges, including poverty, that SMEs activities are supposed to address.

In South Africa, poverty is closely linked to various social and economic challenges. The effects of poverty are exacerbated by inadequate access to essential services, substandard housing, limited job opportunities, and poor infrastructure—issues that have persisted due to the lasting impacts of apartheid. In its inaugural year, the African National Congress (ANC)-led government officially adopted a policy of 'growth through redistribution', which aimed to use a strong state and market to drive growth while also reducing poverty and inequality. However, by 1996, the government shifted towards a conventional neoliberal approach as a core element of its anti-poverty strategy (Cheru, 2001). Local economic development (LED) in post-apartheid South Africa has become a pivotal focus of economic strategies in South Africa (Kontsiwe & Visser, 2019).

6 Concluding Thoughts

The role of SME finance in promoting economic growth and alleviating poverty remains rarely analysed based on accountability. The chapter challenged the implications of ignoring the accountability strategy in the policy document that supports SMEs in South Africa. The significance of small and medium-sized enterprises (SMEs) in a nation's economic development cannot be overstated. They play a crucial role in generating employment, contributing to GDP, fostering innovation, enhancing human resources, and alleviating poverty. Nonetheless, access to credit poses a considerable challenge for accountability on the part of grant holders. It cannot be concluded that there is a causal effect or relationship between the increase in funding for SMEs and their ability to account for the use. Previous studies indicate that SMEs that are not trained and mentored may not perform and, in extension, cannot account for the use of funds. The same goes for a corrupt system, and a local government, in particular, that intentionally misuses funds and does not provide infrastructure that could help SMEs to be productive. Policy review might be needed to examine the criteria for grants, to include the ability to be accountable. This is problematic where policy is narrow and strictly sees funding as transforming disadvantaged groups but ignores accountability. The chapter has found that inadequate risk management, moral hazard, and the potential for adverse selection impede their ability to secure financing. The suggested SMEs Network Fund involves the establishment of a self-managed fund by SMEs, enabling them to finance their operations without relying on collateral and providing access to relatively lower-cost capital (Akorsu & Agyapong, 2012).

Kalane's study (Kalane, 2015) investigates the factors contributing to the failure of small and medium-sized enterprises (SMEs) in the Free State, emphasising the various risks associated with their management and the challenges faced by owners across different sectors. The study focuses on common reasons for business failures, categorising them into managerial, financial, and economic environmental factors. The findings indicated that managerial and financial issues are significant contributors to SME failures. Respondents highlighted a lack of skills in business management, finance, and marketing as considerable obstacles. Furthermore, insufficient business management skills were identified as a critical factor leading to failure, with respondents noting that such deficiencies jeopardised their enterprises. Additionally, the misuse of company resources for personal purposes, along with financial mismanagement—resulting from a lack of prior audits—further contributed to business collapse. The study emphasised the importance of educational qualifications and managerial capabilities in determining the success or failure of SMEs. The study proposed recommendations, calling on the government and other stakeholders to address the challenges and issues faced by SMEs (Ihugba et al., 2014). It can be concluded that issues of accountability and non-performance due to lack of capacity is not peculiar to South Africa but largely a problem of developing countries, such as those in Africa.

References

Abrie, W., & Doussy, E. (2006). Tax compliance obstacles encountered by small and medium enterprises in South Africa. *Meditari: Research Journal of the School of Accounting Sciences, 14*(1), 1–13.

Ackah, J., & Vuvor, S. (2011). *The challenges faced by small & medium enterprises (SMEs) in obtaining credit in Ghana.*

Akorsu, P. K., & Agyapong, D. (2012). *Alternative model for financing SMEs in Ghana.*

Ayandibu, A. O., & Houghton, J. (2017). The role of small and medium scale enterprises in local economic development (LED). *Journal of Business and Retail Management Research, 11*(2).

Bushe, B. (2019). The causes and impact of business failure among small to micro and medium enterprises in South Africa. *Africa's Public Service Delivery and Performance Review, 7*(1), 1–26.

Cheru, F. (2001). Overcoming apartheid's legacy: The ascendancy of neoliberalism in South Africa's anti-poverty strategy. *Third World Quarterly, 22*(4), 505–527.

Chingwaru, T. (2014). *Impact of trade and economic liberalisation policy reforms on the operations of selected small to medium enterprises (SMEs) in Zimbabwe: A comparative study with South Africa's experiences* (Doctoral dissertation). Durban University of Technology.

Clack, W., & Minnaar, A. (2018). Rural crime in South Africa: An exploratory review of 'farm attacks' and stocktheft as the primary crimes in rural areas. *Acta Criminologica: African Journal of Criminology & Victimology, 31*(1), 103–135.

Fatoki, O. (2012). An investigation into the financial management practices of new micro-enterprises in South Africa. *Journal of social sciences, 33*(2), 179–188.

Herrington, M., & Kew, P. (2016). *Global entrepreneurship monitor South Africa report 2015/16: Is South Africa heading for an economic meltdown?* Retrieved March 10, 2024, from https://www.gemconsortium.org/report/gem/south-africa-2015-2016-report?utm.pdf

Ihugba, O. A., Odii, A., & Njoku, A. (2014). Theoretical analysis of entrepreneurship challenges and prospects in Nigeria. *International Letters of Social and Humanistic Sciences, 5*(16), 21–34.

Irene, B. (2017). Women entrepreneurship in South Africa: Understanding the role of competencies in business success. *The Southern African Journal of Entrepreneurship and Small Business Management, 9*(1), 1–9.

Kalane, L. (2015). *Reasons for failure of SMEs in the Free State* (Doctoral dissertation). University of the Free State.

Kato, A. I. (2024). Building resilience and sustainability in small business enterprises through sustainable venture capital investment in sub-Saharan Africa. *Cogent Economics & Finance, 12*(1), 2399760.

Kongolo, M. (2010). Job creation versus job shedding and the role of SMEs in economic development. *African Journal of Business Management, 4*(11), 2288.

Kontsiwe, N., & Visser, G. (2019). Tourism as a vehicle for local economic development in small towns? When things go wrong: The case of Aliwal North, South Africa. *Geo Journal of Tourism and Geosites, 27*(4), 1334–1346.

Krasniqi, B. A. (2010). Are small firms really credit constrained? Empirical evidence from Kosova. *International Entrepreneurship and Management Journal, 6*, 459–479.

Kuzilwa, J. A. (2005). The role of credit for small business success: A study of the National Entrepreneurship Development Fund in Tanzania. *The Journal of Entrepreneurship, 14*(2), 131–161.

Mafundu, R. H., & Mafini, C. (2019). Internal constraints to business performance in black-owned small to medium enterprises in the construction industry. *The Southern African Journal of Entrepreneurship and Small Business Management, 11*(1), 1–10.

Majadibodu, M. J. (2023). Challenges facing small and medium enterprises at the Lephalale local municipality of Limpopo Province in South Africa.

Masutha, M., & Rogerson, C. M. (2015). Business incubation for small enterprise development: South African pathways. In *Urban Forum* (Vol. 26, pp. 223–241). Springer.

Mutegi, H. K., Njeru, P. W., & Ongesa, N. T. (2015). *Financial literacy and its impact on loan repayment by small and medium entrepreneurs.*

Ndege, M., & Park, B. (2015). Factors that affect the growth and development of small, micro, and medium-sized business enterprises in the Vaal triangle region of Gauteng Province in South Africa. *European Journal of Business, Economics and Accountancy, 3*(3), 73–100.

Nkwinika, M. K. K., & Munzhedzi, P. H. (2016). The role of small medium enterprises in the implementation of Local Economic Development in South Africa. South African Association for Public Administration & Management (SAAPAM). Limpopo Chapter Conference Proceedings.

OECD. (2022). *Financing SMEs and entrepreneurs 2022.* https://www.oecd.org/content/dam/oecd/en/publications/reports/2022/03/financing-smes-and-entrepreneurs-2022_f1884241/e9073a0f-en.pdf

Oosthuizen, M., & Thornhill, C. (2017). The grant system of financing the south African local government sphere: Can sustainable local government be promoted? *Local Economy, 32*(5), 433–450.

Perera, D., & Chand, P. (2015). Issues in the adoption of international financial reporting standards (IFRS) for small and medium-sized enterprises (SMEs). *Advances in Accounting, 31*(1), 165–178.

Ramlee, S., & Berma, B. (2013). Financing gap in Malaysian small-medium enterprises: A supply-side perspective. *South African Journal of Economic and Management Sciences, 16*(5), 115–126.

Rogerson, C. M. (2013). Improving market access opportunities for urban small, medium and micro-enterprises in South Africa. *Urbani Izziv, 24*(2), 133–143.

Rogerson, C. M. (2018). The economic development of South Africa's townships. In *The geography of South Africa: Contemporary changes and new directions* (pp. 187–194). Springer International Publishing.

Rudolph, H. P. (2009). *State financial institutions: Mandates, governance, and beyond* (World Bank Policy Research Working Paper No. 5141).

Shackleton, C. M., Blair, A., De Lacy, P., Kaoma, H., Mugwagwa, N., Dalu, M. T., & Walton, W. (2018). How important is green infrastructure in small and medium-sized towns? Lessons from South Africa. *Landscape and Urban Planning, 180*, 273–281.

Shava, E. (2016). Black economic empowerment in South Africa: Challenges and prospects. *Journal of Economics and Behavioral Studies, 8*(6 (J)), 161–170.

Soga, B. V. (2022). *A comparative analysis of the use of e-government services by small businesses* (Doctoral dissertation), University of Johannesburg.

Ssekitoleko, P., & du Plessis, Y. (2021). Unravelling the makings for entrepreneurial success: A case study of the Maponya business in South Africa. *The Southern African Journal of Entrepreneurship and Small Business Management, 13*(1), 424.

The European Commission. (2014). *Small and medium-sized enterprises (SMEs): Closing the gap on business growth.* European Commission. Retrieved May 24, 2024, from https://www.eib.org/files/publications/thematic/sme_report_2014_en.pdf

Yoshino, N., & Taghizadeh Hesary, F. (2016). *Major challenges facing small and medium-sized enterprises in Asia and solutions for mitigating them.*

CHAPTER 6

Partnership for Trust in Government Grant Programmes in South Africa

1 Introduction

The concept of small and medium enterprises (SMEs) and entrepreneurship emerged in the late 1940s, prompting the development of various policies, including grants, subsidised loans, and special tax incentives aimed at supporting SMEs. In addition, governments established small business support agencies to benefit SMEs, with notable initiatives launching in Japan, the United States, India, Tanzania, and Turkey in 1948, 1953, 1954, 1966, and 1976, respectively (Keskin et al., 2010, p. 189). The Organisation for Economic Cooperation and Development (OECD) acknowledges SMEs as essential contributors to the economy and the broader business landscape (OECD, 2022, p. 19). They play a crucial role in advancing the Sustainable Development Goals (SDGs) by promoting inclusive and sustainable economic growth, creating job opportunities, supporting sustainable industrial development, encouraging innovation, and helping to reduce income disparities among nations at various stages of development (OECD, 2017, p. 8). In 2016, the government of Lesotho implemented the Micro, Small, and Medium Enterprises (MSME) policy to address challenges hindering the development of MSMEs in the country (Masupha et al., 2017, p. 7). This policy identified critical issues MSMEs face, such as access to finance, market entry, technological advancement, entrepreneurial training, skills enhancement, infrastructure development, and the establishment of conducive

T. O. Aluko, *Evaluation of Small Business Support in Post-Apartheid South Africa*, https://doi.org/10.1007/978-981-95-2864-6_6

business environments (Molebatsi, 2021, p. 20). However, the evidence of collaboration for innovation in supporting SMEs and evaluating government programmes is not common.

Collaboration holds significant potential to address needs within the public sector effectively. By engaging with entities in the government, private sector, or voluntary sector, collaborative partnerships enable the government to enhance service delivery strategically. This is accomplished by leveraging various stakeholders' core competencies and resources to counter governmental shortcomings and promote social value creation. Utilising the expertise of public servants alongside external stakeholders empowers these partnerships to improve service quality by carefully managing the differences and interdependencies among participants (Taute et al., 2010). Challenges in allocating and utilising grants for business development are noted in the literature. While different countries have adopted ideas to improve their policy, collaborative methods are not usually noticed.

For instance, a study reveals managerial connections have both direct and indirect effects on financial performance, mediated through firm resources. Furthermore, these resources entirely mediate the relationship between inter-firm collaboration and financial performance. However, government support does not significantly impact the financial performance of SMEs (Zulu-Chisanga et al., 2021). This suggests a need for collaboration for improvement purposes.

Set against the broader context of literature, emphasising the necessity of developing and maintaining partnerships, the expected roles of government in supporting entrepreneurship development, as well as small, medium, and micro-enterprises (SMMEs) in South Africa are crucial. According to Brundin et al. (2008) and Leydesdorff (2012), the Triple Helix Model serves as an effective strategy for regional development, enhancing the knowledge economy and fostering entrepreneurship, particularly among micro-enterprises. The study identifies seven key stakeholders involved in partnerships, various models, and processes for initiating partnerships, as well as strategies for maintaining them. Results indicated that partnerships yielded tangible benefits, including financial support, educational opportunities, skills development, workspace provisions, and technological assistance. However, sustainability emerged as a significant concern, with most partnerships lasting only a few months to a year, and very few extending beyond three years. Challenges related to communication, procedural issues, limited stakeholder engagement, and unclear benefits were also observed. The findings of the partnership need to be examined in the context of South African society, where inequality has been a long-standing issue.

2 Partnership and Business Development in an Unequal Society

Before 1994, significant economic power resided with White minorities, while many Black Africans had to resort to working on farms owned by Afrikaners or remain in their rural communities governed by chiefs (Thaba-Nkadimene et al., 2019). One method of oppressing Black individuals during apartheid was to instil the belief that they possessed inferior abilities to pursue complex academic programmes such as engineering, medicine, and other sciences. In a similar vein, the intention was to render Black communities excessively reliant on the future dictated by the colonial government. The period following 1994 saw government initiatives aimed at supporting SMEs across various sectors. The statistics illustrating growth in national income resulting from support for small businesses indicate that adequate funding could directly impact development. However, economists contend that growth in GDP does not necessarily ensure household welfare or development at the grassroots level (Walker et al., 2021). Despite the increase in business activities in South Africa, the poverty level has not significantly diminished in proportion.

During the apartheid era, White minorities did not allow Black people to think independently. They fostered a culture of fear in Black communities (Hocoy, 2020), dictating how they must conform to certain expectations without the freedom to exercise creative thinking and approaches to personal development. Now that democracy has ushered in freedom, the initial pitfall has been the assumption that political freedom equates to economic freedom without a collaborative strategy. Essentially, transformation policies in post-apartheid South Africa did not comprehensively incorporate collaboration within the policy framework. Instead, various consultations were organised to shape a new South Africa, including initiatives aimed at supporting Black individuals in owning or developing businesses, particularly those for disadvantaged women.

The democratic transition in South Africa after 1994 led to the implementation of various measures aimed at addressing the inequalities created during the apartheid era. The government introduced a wide range of legislative and regulatory frameworks designed to tackle socio-economic disparities, persistent poverty, and high unemployment rates. These initiatives aimed to create a favourable environment for local businesses, particularly small, medium, and micro-enterprises (SMMEs) and cooperatives, which were viewed as key drivers of economic development, job creation, and entrepreneurship. The outcome of the policy shows the need for effective partnership to promote business development better. However, South Africa still battles with the effects of apartheid and the society is yet to resolve the challenges of inequality that are still present in resource allocation and distribution. It seems unlikely that the government will improve the system without considering the capacities and expertise of different agencies. Put it differently, there is a need to evaluate government programmes to draw ideas for improvement from both private and public sector organisations.

For instance, the Dr. Kenneth Kaunda District Municipality (Dr KKDM) launched a business grant-funding initiative to support local entrepreneurs and promote business growth. However, it quickly became apparent that Dr. KKDM was disbursing funds without a cohesive funding model to ensure that SMMEs and cooperatives were committed to the ongoing development of their operations. Moreover, there were almost no mechanisms in place to monitor or evaluate the performance of businesses after they received funding, which made it challenging to assess the economic impact of the grants or determine whether taxpayer money was being used effectively. The findings revealed that the current funding approaches faced significant challenges. It is suggested that the model could apply to other district municipalities across the country, thereby contributing to business growth, local economic development, and the overall well-being of communities in South Africa (Rangwetsi, 2021). This shows how testing different models and using different ideas can help to improve funding methods for SMEs in the country. After 30 years of democracy, it appears that an evaluation of government programmes should be undertaken to understand what works and whether it can be refined in different regions to understand the contribution to social and economic development.

Micro, small, and medium enterprises (MSMEs) are widely recognised for their vital contribution to social and economic development. This acknowledgement has prompted numerous countries to integrate MSME development initiatives into national strategies. In South Africa, the post-apartheid administration introduced various developmental policies and established institutions via the Department of Trade and Industry (DTI) to promote the growth of previously marginalised MSMEs. An alarming 85% of MSMEs in South Africa function informally and often operate with a survivalist approach, predominantly located in townships. Regrettably, about 70% of these businesses fail within the first 5 to 7 years, highlighting that the advancement of the MSME sector in South Africa is not achieving the necessary progress, despite the existence of government-led business development services (BDS). It also calls for another approach, which could be a partnership-oriented method to understand the reason for the policy failure of government programmes.

Given these obstacles, a study has explored the advantages and challenges of utilising the development services from the viewpoint of township-based MSMEs. The results revealed several key challenges, including a misalignment between demand and supply, limited access to funding, a lack of aftercare programmes, scepticism towards government services, and insufficient quality. On a positive note, alignment between demand and supply was observed in outsourced training, the quality of financial services was recognised as beneficial, and support for regulatory compliance was found to be extremely valuable. Based on these findings, the study suggests that institutions should emphasise outsourcing training to specialised, sector-specific incubation centres instead of depending solely on in-house training. Development Finance Institutions (DFIs) ought to concentrate on facilitating a transition from the traditional informal sector to a more modernised informal sector rather than pressuring township enterprises to formalise. Additionally, governmental oversight should include formulating policies with measurable objectives that are evaluated on a quarterly basis. Other suggestions entail encouraging consultations, offering mentorship in clusters, creating an alumni network, conducting feedback surveys, ensuring that government services are obtained with legal approval, adopting e-procurement practices, capitalising on public-private partnerships (PPPs), establishing a comprehensive monitoring system, running continuous entrepreneurship campaigns, and embracing an integrated approach.

In a study that examine the support for rural small, medium, and micro-enterprises (SMMEs) in Limpopo Province, South Africa, a survey of 600 SMMEs across six municipal districts in Limpopo sought to understand the characteristics of businesses, evaluate the support systems they require and utilise, and offer recommendations for stakeholders (Ladzani & Netswera, 2009). The complex nature of innovation processes has led to a notable increase in the dependence of small and medium-sized enterprises (SMEs) on external networks.

A study involving 137 Chinese manufacturing SMEs employs structural equation modelling (SEM) to examine the relationship between various cooperative networks and the innovation performance of these enterprises. The results indicate significant positive correlations between inter-firm collaboration, partnerships with intermediary institutions, and cooperation with research organisations, all of which contribute positively to the innovation performance of SMEs. Notably, inter-firm cooperation shows the most pronounced positive impact. In contrast, engagement with government agencies does not significantly affect innovation outcomes. Furthermore, the findings suggest that both vertical and horizontal collaborations with customers, suppliers, and other companies are more critical to the innovation processes of SMEs than horizontal cooperation with educational institutions or government bodies (Zeng et al., 2010).

2.1 Partnership with SMEs for a Better Society

The impact of SMEs in the post-apartheid South is more profound in how it helped the country generate employment from the grassroots and consequently reduced poverty to a certain level. However, the rate of unemployment and poverty in recent years shows different figures or pointed negative effects of the policies of transformation. Looking at the macroeconomic development of South Africa from a SMEs perspective, there is a need to calculate whether these sectors contribute more or continue to impact employment and poverty in the country. However, this has changed in the last 30 years, though the margin of change is not enough to assume that businesses, particularly in rural areas, can produce results when given grants without training and other forms of support. For instance, how could policymakers expect businesses and business owners in rural communities to research and conduct feasibility studies about their business without technical support? Many recommendations addressing business failure since democracy highlight a significant lack of awareness regarding relevant policies and contexts.

Poverty metrics reinforce the widely held view that the Free State, for instance, is one of the most impoverished provinces in South Africa, particularly highlighting the challenges faced by Qwaqwa. While government assistance to alleviate poverty may provide short-term benefits, often leading to violent protests, a more effective strategy might involve offering entrepreneurship training and essential resources. Such initiatives could empower owners of micro and small enterprises (MSEs) to grow their businesses and break free from poverty. Moreover, a study shows that MSE operators in Phuthaditjhaba, the commercial centre of Qwaqwa, often remain unaware of the government resources available to support small business owners, primarily due to significant communication barriers. Despite their financial limitations, MSE owners have identified critical support areas that could foster growth, including access to funding, government aid, infrastructure, training, and appropriate premises (Mensah & Benedict, 2010). Partnerships with different government agencies, NGOS, and industries that support and promote awareness of business development are necessary to bridge the gap between government opportunities and access to these opportunities. Effective modelling based on the challenges can improve the distribution of government resources to SMEs and, most importantly, is likely to reduce challenges related to social problems, including violence, in this region. Though the study has not established this, the assumption is that society creates peace when business enterprises thrive. However, this cannot be done in isolation. All forms of partnerships are needed for society, particularly for young people to become agents of societal development.

On the other hand, there is compelling evidence suggesting that young entrepreneurs in Sub-Saharan Africa often create start-up businesses in isolation. They face significant pressure and lack connections to the broader entrepreneurial ecosystem, contributing to high failure rates among these ventures. Key players in this ecosystem—such as educational institutions, industry partners, and investors—possess valuable knowledge and resources, both human and financial, that could provide essential technical and market support to these young entrepreneurs. However, despite the presence of these important stakeholders, collaboration among them appears weak and needs strengthening for 'job seekers' to effectively become 'job creators'.

Thus, there is a pressing need for a strategy to develop functional multi-stakeholder partnerships that can nurture thriving ecosystems supportive of young entrepreneurs in Africa. A study outlines various strategies from the Nexus Project aimed at enhancing the entrepreneurship ecosystem for young entrepreneurs in Nigeria, facilitating their evolution from 'locked' to 'unlocked', and ultimately to 'investable' entrepreneurs. The findings indicate that cultivating functional ecosystems within the African context requires a collective vision and engagement grounded in shared values among stakeholders. Aligning a subset of stakeholders around a common objective improved access to a broader range of ecosystem members, resulting in effective interactions and beneficial outcomes for young start-up founders. Young people are instrumental in determining a peaceful society. If they receive adequate support, there is a greater possibility of achieving a better society. Meanwhile, supporting young people's businesses necessitates a unique partnership to be effective. There is a clear relationship between the rate of businesses owned by young people and their impact on economic growth, which in turn can reduce crime rates within the country. In other words, crime rates will likely follow as unemployment rises and youth disengage from policies that support businesses. A significant proportion of crimes are committed by young men. If the government continues to prioritise funding for young people's businesses, curbing crime will likely remain a significant challenge. Therefore, resourcing young people's businesses cannot disproportionately focus on women in countries such as South Africa, where young men also need to be actively engaged for economic security, transformation, and stability. The positive ripple effect of shared values that guided initial partnerships within the broader ecosystem illustrates that silos can be dismantled when stakeholders take the initiative (Adewale et al., 2025).

2.2 *Partnership to Address Financial Challenges by SMEs*

The criteria for granting finance to SMEs should demonstrate fairness in terms of whether a business contributes to the environment, develops skills, and/or supports regional development. Likewise, the business' individuals or team should provide details on how the funds will be utilised. It is not just to provide substantial funding to a team that lacks experience in managing a business or has a poor reputation for handling finances. The non-financial value enhances other aspects, ultimately leading to profits and growth, as turnover must increase over time. However, negative feedback can adversely affect a business. This indicates that soft skills play a crucial role for SMEs, as negative feedback can impact the business' reputation and growth. SMEs have a social responsibility and are accountable to taxpayers, who enable the government to provide interventions in the form of social grants or funding. This means that the value a business creates, alongside non-financial value, has a direct implication for the social justice concerning the utilisation of taxpayers' money. Consequently, SMEs must create a positive experience for customers to remain in business and provide justification for the funds allocated to them.

In South Africa, government regulatory bodies are responsible for monitoring business activities, including granting permits to businesses that offer sensitive services such as healthcare. Compliance is required for all businesses, including small enterprises. While small businesses within specific profit brackets may not be subject to taxation, other requirements remain mandatory depending on the type of business. Competition will not cease, particularly in lucrative sectors and industries that are profitable. Consequently, only businesses that comply with government regulations and operate within the legal framework will be able to establish a reputation in the market and grow. The reasons some SMEs go out of business include non-compliance and the inability to access information regarding compliance requirements. This factor highlights the potential for policy to further support SMEs in remaining operational and justify using grants as a result.

The issue of financing for small and medium-sized enterprises (SMEs) is complex and should be treated as a priority. While SMEs need to seek solutions to their financial challenges actively, their capabilities are often limited, highlighting the critical role that other stakeholders in the financial sector play. In this context, governments must take on a significant responsibility, as they can serve as a catalyst, investor, and regulator, thereby reinforcing the economy's supply side. For example, a study examines how the Government of Botswana (GoB) can effectively facilitate SME financing. The research suggests four financing options that the GoB might consider: direct financial assistance schemes, loan guarantee programmes, direct credit grant initiatives, and funding for technical and managerial advisory services. Stakeholders need to assess these options based on their economic viability before proceeding with implementation (Tesfayohannes, 2012). On the other hand, there might be a need to approach financial solutions from multiple partnership approaches to ensure that models that finance SMEs are continually improved for sustainability purposes.

While collaboration is essential to address the problem of governance and performance in public sector organisations, their nature partnership and its dimensions are equally important. For instance, partnership with the Development Bank of Southern Africa (DBSA) and similar entities can provide access to more funds in different forms and capacity-building opportunities (SEDA, 2021). However, this regional partnership should be used to build transparent, innovative business solutions in South Africa. There are innovative ideas within Southern African countries that can be benchmarked and need collaboration. This type of project should be funded by DBSA and similar entities. In Asia, Small Industries Development Bank (SIDBI) and Malaysia's SME Bank are performing similar functions, especially in building capacity (OECD, 2020). There is a need to compare practices and to learn about different initiatives that have resulted in success in both Asia and Southern Africa.

Also, Sustainable entrepreneurship (SE) is becoming increasingly important globally, yet our understanding of its dynamics, especially within small and medium-sized enterprises (SMEs) in South Africa, remains limited. Previous research has often neglected to consider how contextual factors influence the sustainability of these SMEs. A study has found that SME characteristics, government support, management skills, positive employee-employer relationships, and start-up capital are all linked to sustainable entrepreneurship. Entrepreneurs and business partners need to continuously seek innovative ideas that align with SME characteristics. They will need to also promote a proactive approach among their employees and manage risks associated with high-stakes ventures, which can lead to financial success. There is an urgent need for comprehensive interventions to strengthen the SME sector, which is a crucial driver of economic development and equity. The South African government, along with other developing nations, needs to commit to creating an environment that promotes sustainability in entrepreneurship (Ogujiuba et al., 2020).

2.3 Multi-Layer Partnership for SMEs Transformation

In the context of South Africa and according to the definition provided by the National Small Business Act of 1996, small business is characterised by company turnover, size, and sector (Kganyago, 2022). Similarly, small and medium enterprises (SMEs) have been regarded as important factors for development in many countries. They have played a significant role in supporting rural businesses and local economic growth in the Czech Republic (Abrham et al., 2015). The development of small businesses is a critical success factor for construction companies in Iran (Sarvari et al.,

2021). Germany is considered the fastest-growing economy in Europe and its growth can also be attributed to the significance of SMEs for development (Herr & Nettekoven, 2018). Therefore, SMEs with effective policies have been employed in developed and developing nations to achieve economic prosperity and alleviate poverty. Following 1994, SMEs were identified in South Africa as a key area of focus for transformative economic development (Rens et al., 2021). In terms of policies, the activities of SMEs are anticipated to contribute to job creation, economic growth, and innovation in South Africa. Statistically, SMEs in South Africa contribute significantly to the Gross Domestic Product (GDP) and employment (Pulka & Gawuna, 2022). Over recent decades, their contribution accounts for approximately 34% of South Africa's GDP. Regarding employment growth, SMEs have been responsible for about 60% of total employment in the country since 1994.

A way to predict performance is to examine how financial support for SMEs in different provinces produces results for development. While national measurements of performance and future predictions are vital, performance variables can also be modelled to understand how businesses in different provinces contribute to the overall development of South Africa. However, development must be defined. In South Africa, development is narrowly defined, specifically around racial groups and occasionally encompassing gender, which indicates that race is a crucial factor in modelling the performance and contributions of SMEs to the economic development of South Africa. Another consideration is the outcome of the financial support provided by the government, which is outlined in the policy that establishes or commissions funding or grants for the government. This policy document primarily seeks to achieve transformation through grants and assumes that when the government allocates funds to SMEs, there should be a corresponding impact on reducing poverty and unemployment. Poverty and high unemployment have been two significant issues facing South Africa since 1994, with little change. Literature findings link quality and corruption as primary reasons for these challenges. However, it is unknown how SMEs may have altered or failed to alter the impact of these issues. If SMEs have contributed, there is also a need to measure the level or percentage of their contribution to poverty reduction and unemployment.

The government has supported different categories of business owners since 1994. One such category includes young people who choose to become entrepreneurs due to their inability to pass high school or lack of opportunity to attend formal schooling. Another category comprises young individuals who, after completing high school or even university education, find themselves unable to secure employment and decide to try their hand at business. These two categories differ in educational background, but age is a common factor. In other words, they are young people who are likely to possess skills in technology and networking, although this largely depends on the environment in which they were raised. The prevailing notion is that young people of this generation benefit from technological advantages and exposures that were not available to older generations. This is what the government aims to leverage to stimulate business activities and boost the economy of South Africa. However, whether age, with or without formal education at various levels, determines business success is a research question that warrants modelling, analysis, and discussion.

Different political parties have advocated for addressing genuine issues surrounding social justice rather than merely skimming the surface. The challenge with social justice lies in its dependence on politics and the political will to tackle what the majority of the population perceives as problems in their daily lives. When the government introduced programmes for SMEs, South Africa held hope of attaining justice from economic oppression and achieving economic freedom by 2030 (Hassen et al., 2018). However, the concept of justice should be absolute, not partial. By absolute, it is meant that SMEs should feel empowered not solely through financial assistance to start a business. They also desire the freedom to access other opportunities, such as acquiring business premises without exclusion, and the ability to engage in business sectors that historically belonged to White individuals without facing discrimination, alongside several other factors that would foster a sense of justice. Nevertheless, the government has a regulatory role to achieve economic freedom through small business financing (Graafland & Gerlagh, 2019). In other words, everyone, regardless of race, should have the freedom to conduct business they are capable of without facing discrimination. When individuals do not feel a sense of belonging in a particular business space or are excluded due to their economic status, this represents partial justice. One might assume that policies are in place to ensure social justice in business activities in South Africa. However, cases of exclusion persist, leaving Black individuals feeling economically disadvantaged.

In a different context, while many studies have focused on empowering marginalised individuals to advocate for healthier living conditions, less attention has been given to creating social environments where those in power listen to these voices. Collaboration among small and medium-sized enterprises (SMEs) has emerged as a strategy to enhance industrial competitiveness. Initially recognised in Western Europe, various government agencies and private organisations have tested policies aimed at promoting inter-firm collaboration, commonly referred to as manufacturing networks. The underlying belief behind these policies is that fostering cooperative behaviour among SMEs will improve their competitive edge, which in turn encourages enterprises to change their behaviours and engage in collaboration. These strategies are part of a broader national initiative to drive industrial modernisation through diverse interventions.

Legislators and government bodies investing in network initiatives seek to evaluate their effectiveness and understand their impact on state, regional, and national economies. Despite the relatively small scale of investments, expectations for these initiatives are substantial. For instance, the first evaluation, commissioned by the Oregon Economic Development Department, was conducted at an early stage and focused on processes and industry reactions. The second evaluation, conducted over a three-year grant period for the Northwest Area Foundation, included assessments of changes among participating SMEs. Both evaluations highlight the challenges of linking small, indirect interventions to significant business and economic changes (Rosenfeld, 1996).

Additionally, poverty alleviation has become a priority on the international development agenda, especially following the establishment of the United Nations Millennium Development Goals (MDGs) in 2000. African nations have embarked on various initiatives aimed at achieving sustained economic growth through enhanced productivity, ultimately aimed at reducing poverty. The critical role of SMEs in fostering poverty reduction and creating jobs is widely recognised. Although many SMEs in Africa face high failure rates, some have demonstrated remarkable success, showing growth, innovation, and sustainability. Thus, research has encouraged African governments to prioritise SME development and provide guidance on effectively integrating this development into their poverty alleviation strategies (Abisuga-Oyekunle et al., 2020).

3 Innovation in Partnership to Support SMEs Development

The resources and capabilities of enterprises are essential for achieving a competitive edge. However, many enterprises face significant challenges related to innovation, including disadvantages linked to their size and age, as well as entry barriers. As a result, an increasing number of enterprises are adopting innovation practices that leverage both internal and external knowledge flows to foster partnerships with commercial and scientific agents for innovation exploration and exploitation. In this context, universities may play a crucial role by providing knowledge-rich environments that nurture the development of innovative and entrepreneurial ideas. This approach is observed in emerging economies like Mexico, where governments have established subsidies to promote enterprise innovation through mandatory partnerships with universities. This study has examined the motivations of Mexican enterprises to partner with universities for innovation objectives—both exploration and exploitation—as well as their options for accessing public funds, such as the required university partnerships. The findings demonstrate the significant impact of universities on enterprises' exploratory innovation practices and their access to R&D research subsidies (Guerrero et al., 2019).

After the end of apartheid in 1994, the African National Congress (ANC) initially focused on national reconciliation, which allowed its approach to Black Economic Empowerment (BEE) to seem non-threatening to White interests. However, the government's current strategy has shifted to a more proactive stance, aimed at cultivating a Black capitalist class that is both loyal and productive, as articulated in the ANC's framework for the 'National Democratic Revolution'. In response, corporate interests are starting to recognise BEE's necessity and potential benefits. Nevertheless, given the significant role of the state in promoting Black capitalism, there are considerable risks of it devolving into a system of cronyism akin to that observed in certain Asian economies. Consequently, the concept of patriotic Black capitalism stands at odds with its potential exploitative tendencies (Southall, 2004).

While a section of the literature ignores other factors that could be responsible for business success aside from grants, there is evidence that government support for business could aid economic prosperity. Whether the grant scheme for small businesses is designed to accommodate systemic issues in South African society is a question of politics and policies. This chapter deconstructs different aspects of government financial support schemes, framing them from stakeholders' theory. The analysis includes whether the purposes of grants include informing, satisfying political intention, or fundamental development. The literature and empirical findings of studies focusing on the impact of government support since 1994 provide counterintuitive data to make a case for strengthening the business ecosystem from evidence-based policy.

In other words, we cannot enforce social justice forcefully, especially when policies have already made provisions for it. Social justice can be subtle, but policies amplify its effects by creating more opportunities for Black South Africans, particularly women. One of the key elements of social justice is inclusivity. Not only is the policy imbalanced, but it has also excluded and ignored the country's diversity since 1994. There may be alternative ways to redirect such a policy to achieve absolute social justice and inclusion (Sisk, 2017). The tension within the business sector and the persistent violence surrounding opportunities, particularly in the agriculture and mining industries, is a result of imbalanced policies.

There is consistent recognition of reconciliation and an attempt to create peace in the policies. Thus, social justice can sometimes be likened to sharing a plate of food, but with certain individuals allowed to eat first and be satisfied before others can partake. This is how disadvantaged people perceive social justice in South Africa and, to some extent, in other countries. Everyone should have equal opportunities to share the same plate without depriving anyone of their right to participate in the meal. The argument posits that some individuals may eat faster, or the food may not even meet their needs, rendering it pointless to share a plate. This presents a challenge for the government. They are confronted with the decision to serve different meals to different people living in the same country while still ensuring that the process is equitable and just.

Literature indicates that many small businesses did not survive for more than three months. The only option for the government is to identify ways to seek assistance from large businesses to support struggling small businesses. This situation largely depends on the ruling political parties and whether they are influenced by wealthy individuals who may be reluctant to pay high taxes. Consequently, the widening inequality serves as evidence of the presence of social justice, which aligns closely with the Keynesian theory regarding taxation and government intervention in the market as a means of wealth redistribution.

3.1 *Immigrant Entrepreneurship*

Another interesting perspective is immigrant entrepreneurship in terms of importance and the obstacles faced in managing micro-enterprises. A study shows that while xenophobia is not a widespread concern for African foreign entrepreneurs in Cape Town, it presents a significant risk to their businesses. Furthermore, limited proficiency in local languages emerged as a notable challenge. Entrepreneurs reported fluctuations in sales and contended with intense competition from numerous similar businesses in the area. Access to funding for both start-up and expansion continues to be a significant hurdle for these micro-enterprises. Additionally, securing suitable business premises is challenging due to high rental costs and crime rates. The study concludes with recommendations for immigrant entrepreneurs and relevant government departments aimed at alleviating the challenges faced by African foreign entrepreneurs managing micro-enterprises (Khosa & Kalitanyi, 2014).

In July 2021, civil unrest dramatically affected the primary economic sectors in two provinces of South Africa. During this time, thousands of demonstrators vandalised shopping centres across various cities and towns. Both small and large businesses faced rampant looting and arson, resulting in widespread chaos throughout many communities. Critical national highways were obstructed, and trucks were deliberately set ablaze to disrupt economic activities. This turmoil resulted in over 300 fatalities, escalated unemployment rates, and significant damage to infrastructure. Small businesses, already struggling to recover from the effects of COVID-19, were disproportionately impacted as most lacked insurance and the means to recover swiftly. The unrest underscored the severe strain on South Africa's public administration and highlighted the growing divide between the affluent and the impoverished. Enhanced accountability, trust, and political commitment are essential to facilitate recovery and bolster resilience among small businesses in the short and long term.

These challenges are expected to significantly impact small enterprises, particularly micro, rural, and township businesses that lack adequate resources for a complete recovery. Furthermore, rising inflation, increasing fuel and electricity costs, and soaring prices of basic goods will likely obstruct recovery efforts, undermining the resilience and sustainability of numerous businesses in the coming years. South Africa's economic performance has recently declined due to recession, political mismanagement, and a lack of accountability, resulting in heightened unemployment, poverty, and inequality. Collaborative efforts from the business community are vital to tackling these challenges. (Makhaye & Subban, SSIRC 2022–2025).

4 Concluding Remarks

Partnerships between the state and civil society in the context of effective policy implementation emphasise key factors that contribute to their success. These factors include the clear definition of objectives and ensuring alignment, establishing mechanisms for collaboration and coordination, clarifying roles and responsibilities, and possessing the capacity to fulfil those duties. Governments need to enhance the efficacy of collaborations between the state and civil society (Brinkerhoff, 1999). Meanwhile, a study has revealed that small businesses primarily struggle due to insufficient government and entrepreneurial support, as well as prevalent corruption. However, SMEs highlighted that educational resources, small business support platforms, and government systems are the most beneficial services that smart cities could provide. Various literary sources were referenced to connect these smart city services with the business challenges they could potentially alleviate. They also examined the necessary infrastructure for each service to identify possible dependencies and implementation challenges. The study consolidated its findings to develop a roadmap aimed at enhancing smart city services for small business support. This roadmap serves as a guide for cities in strategising their smart city initiatives to better assist small businesses in fulfilling their crucial role in the economy (Du Plessis & Marnewick, 2017).

There are lessons to learn from the intention of South Africa's policy on the SME sector and its implementation in practice. The policy intends to redress inequality and redistribute wealth after 1994. The expectation is that when this policy is implemented, it will reduce poverty, unemployment, and the crime rate in the country. After 1994 or 30 years of democracy, it seems that unemployment, poverty, and crime rates have increased drastically. It appears that the policy is not working, or the process for implementing it needs review for effectiveness. Compared to other countries that have implemented successful programmes for small businesses, South Africa can learn that the policy of transformation needs to be fit not only to the context but also be designed to include all the factors that will ensure real transformation and development. These factors mean to embrace the current trend brought by digital transformation, focusing on and funding businesses that will bring solutions to the South African economy and society. It means policy will not just fund businesses based on race alone, but business owners or proposals will have criteria that encourage solutions to critical issues in the South African economy. Essentially, one big lesson is accountability. Countries like South Korea and others make sure that there is a feedback channel in the policy that funds SMEs. In other words, the use of funds is accounted for, and where there are deficiencies, policies are reviewed. It appears that this lesson will be useful to rethink the purpose and/ or goals of financing business in South Africa. In the context of South Africa, businesses in rural communities may not be able to comply with the digital technologies' requirements in filing requirements. This is a big gap that the South African government needs to close by creating training programmes for business owners in this category. The training will include financial or business literacy, technology use, and reporting compliance. Herrington & Kwe (2016) recommend that private industries, such as MTN, for instance, can assist the government in building capacities that will make small businesses grow.

References

Abisuga-Oyekunle, O. A., Patra, S. K., & Muchie, M. (2020). SMEs in sustainable development: Their role in poverty reduction and employment generation in sub-Saharan Africa. *African Journal of Science, Technology, Innovation and Development, 12*(4), 405–419.

Abrham, J., Strielkowski, W., Vošta, M., & Šlajs, J. (2015). Factors that influence the competitiveness of Czech rural small and medium enterprises. *Agricultural Economics/Zemědělská Ekonomika, 61*(10).

Adewale, A., Okupe, A., Immanuel, S., Choulet, J. P., Van Zyl, B., & Bizama, A. P. (2025). An approach to developing functional multi-stakeholder partnerships for entrepreneurship ecosystem development: A case study of the Nexus Project. In *Developing university entrepreneurial ecosystems in sub-Saharan Africa* (pp. 227–253).

Brinkerhoff, D. W. (1999). Exploring state–civil society collaboration: Policy partnerships in developing countries. *Nonprofit and Voluntary Sector Quarterly, 28*(1_suppl), 59–86.

Brundin, E., Patzelt, H., & Shepherd, D. A. (2008). Managers' emotional displays and employees' willingness to act entrepreneurially. *Journal of Business Venturing, 23*(2), 221–243.

Du Plessis, H., & Marnewick, A. (2017). A roadmap for smart city services to address challenges faced by small businesses in South Africa. *South African Journal of Economic and Management Sciences, 20*(1), 1–18.

Graafland, J., & Gerlagh, R. (2019). Economic freedom, internal motivation, and corporate environmental responsibility of SMEs. *Environmental and Resource Economics, 74*(3), 1101–1123.

Guerrero, M., Urbano, D., & Herrera, F. (2019). Innovation practices in emerging economies: Do university partnerships matter? *The Journal of Technology Transfer, 44*, 615–646.

Hassen, S., Gebrehiwot, T., & Arega, T. (2018). Determinants of enterprises use of energy efficient technologies: Evidence from urban Ethiopia. *Energy Policy, 119*, 388–395.

Herr, H., & Nettekoven, Z. M. (2018). *The role of small and medium-sized enterprises in development: What can be learned from the German experience?* (Working Paper No. 53). Global Labour University.

Herrington, M., & Kew, P. (2016). *Global entrepreneurship monitor South Africa report 2015/16: Is South Africa heading for an economic meltdown?* Retrieved March 10, 2024, from https://www.gemconsortium.org/report/gem/south-africa-2015-2016-report?utm.pdf

Hocoy, D. (2020). Marginalization among blacks in South Africa. In *Latest contributions to cross-cultural psychology* (pp. 88–103). Routledge.

Keskin, H., Şentürk, C., Sungur, O., & Kiriş, H. M. (2010, June 8–9). The importance of SMEs in developing economies. *Paper presented at the 2nd International Symposium on Sustainable Development (ISSD'10)*, Sarajevo, Bosnia-Herzegovina.

Kganyago, M. M. (2022). *Business tourism organisations in South Africa: A strategic integrated communication approach (SIC)* (Doctoral dissertation). North-West University.

Khosa, R. M., & Kalitanyi, V. (2014). Challenges in operating micro-enterprises by African foreign entrepreneurs in Cape Town, South Africa. *Mediterranean Journal of Social Sciences, 5*(10), 205–215.

Ladzani, W., & Netswera, G. (2009). Support for rural small businesses in Limpopo Province, South Africa. *Development Southern Africa, 26*(2), 225–239.

Leydesdorff, L. (2012). The triple helix, quadruple helix,..., and an N-tuple of helices: explanatory models for analyzing the knowledge-based economy? *Journal of the knowledge economy, 3*(1), 25–35.

Masupha, L. P., Beharry-Ramraj, A., & Amolo, J. (2017). State financial assistance within Lesotho Maseru's small, medium and micro enterprises. *Public and Municipal Finance, 6*(4), 7–14.

Mensah, S. A., & Benedict, E. (2010). Entrepreneurship training and poverty alleviation: Empowering the poor in the eastern Free State of South Africa. *African Journal of Economic and Management Studies, 1*(2), 138–163.

Molebatsi, M. B. (2021). *Effectiveness of institutional mechanisms on small businesses in Mokhotlong and Qacha's Nek, Lesotho* (Doctoral dissertation, Master's dissertation). University of Kwazulu-Natal. Available at: https://researchspace.ukzn.ac.za/handle/10413/20080

OECD. (2017). *Enhancing the contributions of SMEs in a global and digitalised economy (C/MIN(2017)8/FINAL).* Meeting of the OECD Council at Ministerial Level. Retrieved June 10, 2024, from https://www.oecd.org/industry/CMIN-2017-8-EN.pdf

OECD. (2022). *Financing SMEs and entrepreneurs 2022: An OECD scoreboard.* OECD Publishing. Retrieved June 9, 2024, from https://www.oecd.org/en/publications/financing-smes-and-entrepreneurs-2022_e9073a0fen.html

Ogujiuba, K. K., Boshoff, E., Agholor, A. I., & Olamide, E. G. (2020). SMEs and sustainable entrepreneurship in South Africa: Impact analysis of contextual factors in the services sector. *Business Administration and Business Economics.*

Pulka, B. M., & Gawuna, M. S. (2022). Contributions of SMEs to employment, gross domestic product, economic growth and development. *Jalingo Journal of Social and Management Sciences, 4*(1), 1–18.

Rangwetsi, M. R. (2021). *A funding model framework for SMMEs and Cooperatives: The case of Dr. Kenneth Kaunda District Municipality* (Doctoral dissertation). North-West University.

Rens, V., Iwu, C. G., Tengeh, R. K., & Esambe, E. E. (2021). SMEs, economic growth, and business incubation conundrum in South Africa. A literature appraisal. *Journal of Management and Research, 8*(2), 214–251.

Rosenfeld, S. A. (1996). Does cooperation enhance competitiveness? Assessing the impacts of inter-firm collaboration. *Research Policy, 25*(2), 247–263.

Sarvari, H., Chan, D. W., Alaeos, A. K. F., Olawumi, T. O., & Aldaud, A. A. A. (2021). Critical success factors for managing construction small and medium-sized enterprises in developing countries of Middle East: Evidence from Iranian construction enterprises. *Journal of Building Engineering, 43*, 103152.

SEDA (Small Enterprise Development Agency). (2021). *SMME quarterly update: 1st quarter 2021.* SEDA. Retrieved March 11, 2024, from https://www.seda.org.za/Publications/Publications/SMME%20Quarterly%202021%20Q1%20September.pdf

Sisk, T. D. (2017). *Democracy and resilience: Conceptual approaches and considerations* (Background Paper for The Global State of Democracy 2017). International IDEA. Retrieved January 4, 2024, from https://www.idea.int/gsod-2017/files/IDEA-GSOD-2017-BACKGROUND-PAPER-RESILIENCE.pdf

Southall, R. (2004). The ANC & black capitalism in South Africa. *Review of African Political Economy, 31*(100), 313–328.

Taute, H. A., Huhmann, B. A., & Thakur, R. (2010). Emotional information management: Concept development and measurement in public service announcements. *Psychology & Marketing, 27*(5), 417–444.

Tesfayohannes, M. (2012). Streamlining government financing programs for SMEs in the sub-Saharan Africa: The case of Botswana. *China-USA Business Review, 11*(2).

Thaba-Nkadimene, K. L., Molotja, W., & Mafumo, T. N. (2019). The scourge of poverty among South African rural women: In defence of social justice. *Journal of Gender, Information and Development in Africa, 8*(3), 69–89.

Walker, C. C., Druckman, A., & Jackson, T. (2021). Welfare systems without economic growth: A review of the challenges and next steps for the field. *Ecological Economics, 186*, 107066.

Zeng, S. X., Xie, X. M., & Tam, C. M. (2010). Relationship between cooperation networks and innovation performance of SMEs. *Technovation, 30*(3), 181–194.

Zulu-Chisanga, S., Chabala, M., & Mandawa-Bray, B. (2021). The varied effects of government assistance, inter-firm collaboration, and firm resources on SME performance in a developing economy. *Journal of Entrepreneurship in Emerging Economies, 13*(2), 175–195.

Correction to: Evaluation of Small Business Support in Post-Apartheid South Africa

Correction to:
T. O. Aluko, *Evaluation of Small Business Support in Post-Apartheid South Africa*, https://doi.org/10.1007/978-981-95-2864-6

The original version of chapter 2 and 4 were inadvertently published with missing sources of few tables and figures, which has now been corrected. The erratum chapter has been updated with the change.

The updated versions of these chapters can be found at
https://doi.org/10.1007/978-981-95-2864-6_2
https://doi.org/10.1007/978-981-95-2864-6_4

T. O. Aluko, *Evaluation of Small Business Support in Post-Apartheid South Africa*, https://doi.org/10.1007/978-981-95-2864-6_7

Index

T. O. Aluko, *Evaluation of Small Business Support in Post-Apartheid South Africa*, https://doi.org/10.1007/978-981-95-2864-6

FSC
www.fsc.org
MIX
Papier | Fördert
gute Waldnutzung
FSC® C083411

Kolibri 360 GmbH
Ferdinand-Jühlke-Straße 7
99095 Erfurt, Deutschland
produktsicherheit@kolibri360.de